Massacred for Gold

"There is so little to know and I think what was known was forgotten."

Marjorie Martin
Former Wallowa County clerk, Enterprise, Oregon

Map courtesy of Oregon Historical Quarterly *and Dean Shapiro*

Massacred for Gold

THE CHINESE IN HELLS CANYON

R. Gregory Nokes

Oregon State University Press
Corvallis

The paper in this book meets the guidelines for permanence and durability
of the Committee on Production Guidelines for Book Longevity of the
Council on Library Resources and the minimum requirements of the
American National Standard for Permanence of Paper for Printed Library
Materials Z39.48-1984.

Library of Congress Cataloging-in-Publication Data
Nokes, R. Gregory.
  Massacred for gold : the Chinese in Hells Canyon / by R. Gregory Nokes.
    p. cm.
  Includes bibliographical references and index.
  ISBN 978-0-87071-570-9 (alk. paper)
  1. Snake River Massacre, 1887. 2. Chinese Americans--Crimes against
--Hells Canyon (Idaho and Or.)--History--19th century. 3. Gold miners
--Hells Canyon (Idaho and Or.)--History--19th century. 4. Immigrants--
Hells Canyon (Idaho and Or.)--History--19th century. 5. Massacres--Hells
Canyon (Idaho and Or.)--History--19th century. 6. Murder--Hells Canyon
(Idaho and Or.)--History--19th century. 7. Racism--Hells Canyon (Idaho
and Or.)--History--19th century. 8. Hells Canyon (Idaho and Or.)--Race
relations--History--19th century. 9. Hells Canyon (Idaho and Or.)--
History--19th century. 10. Snake River Valley (Wyo.-Wash.)--History--
19th century. I. Title.
  F882.H44N65 2009
  979.5'73041--dc22
                                    2009008651

Oregon State University Press
121 The Valley Library
Corvallis OR 97331-4501
541-737-3166 • fax 541-737-3170
http://oregonstate.edu/dept/press

To Candise:

Your love and encouragement helped make this book possible.

TABLE OF CONTENTS

Prologue

WE KNOW ONLY these eleven names:

Chea Po
Chea Sun
Chea Yow
Chea Shun
Chea Cheong
Chea Ling
Chea Chow
Chea Lin-chung
Kong Mun-kow
Kong Nhan[1]
Ah Yow[2]

ALL MEN, these eleven were among as many as thirty-four Chinese gold miners robbed and killed on the Oregon side of Hells Canyon in a massacre that began on May 25, 1887. We know little else about them. Of the other two dozen victims, we don't even have their names.

The miners, immigrants from China, were never part of the American Dream. They lived largely anonymous to the Caucasians around them, and died anonymous. Even the burial places for most are unknown—if they were buried at all.

The killers were a gang of rustlers and schoolboys from northeastern Oregon in what is now Wallowa County. Protected by family and friends, some were tried for murder and declared innocent, while the alleged ringleaders fled and were never caught. One would later live a prosperous life in nearby Idaho, quite possibly bankrolled by gold stolen from the Chinese and others.

In lives lost, the Hells Canyon massacre was the worst crime committed by whites against the approximately three hundred thousand Chinese who immigrated to the United States during the latter half of the nineteenth century.[3] But the crime was by no means unique. Violence and discrimination against the Chinese was widespread throughout the American West in the

1870s and 1880s, stemming partly from complaints they took jobs from white workers, and partly from blatant racism, fueled by demagogues.

The irony is that many were welcomed when they first arrived, relieving a serious shortage of labor. They came chiefly to mine gold and build the new railroads then spanning the West. Many also found jobs as farm workers, common laborers, and domestics. But when there was no longer a labor shortage, pressure mounted on the government to send them home.

Congress pandered to the growing anti-Chinese sentiment by enacting the Chinese Exclusion Act of 1882, which barred additional laborers from immigrating—although allowing those already in the country to remain. It was an earlier version of the debate that rages today over the status of undocumented Latino immigrants. The initial period of exclusion was for ten years, but it later continued well into the twentieth century. However, the Act settled nothing. Many of the worst outrages against the Chinese occurred after 1882.

Never fully investigated, the Hells Canyon massacre was all but forgotten until a county clerk in Wallowa County, Oregon, discovered a handful of documents relating to the crime in an unused safe where they had laid hidden for decades. These documents and other discoveries, including recollections of the crime in histories written by two early northeastern Oregon settlers, make it possible for the first time to unravel much of the mystery of what really occurred in Hells Canyon in 1887.

I FIRST LEARNED of the documents found in the safe while I was a reporter for *The Oregonian* of Portland. At the time, I approached the discovery as a news story. But as someone educated in Oregon schools, I wondered why I had never heard of the massacre, certainly one of the worst crimes in the state's history. I was soon to discover the reasons: one, people in Wallowa County, both then and now, didn't want the story told, and, two, authorities at all levels of government—federal, state, and county—cared so little about the Chinese that they made at best only a half-hearted attempt to investigate. As I delved further into the story, I learned that other documents about the case had disappeared, and that long-time county residents who had some knowledge of the massacre proved reluctant to talk. All the evidence pointed to a cover-up extending for more than a century.

What started out as the pursuit of a compelling news story soon became much more. I resolved to break through the silence, and bring the story out of the shadows to take its rightful place as part— albeit a disturbing part—of the remembered history of Oregon and the American West. My efforts took time, years, in fact. Friends and family said they admired my passion. But I wondered whether they weren't being patronizing and, in truth, thought I had become obsessed. And maybe to some extent, I was.

I retired from the newspaper in 2003, which made it easier to find the time to run down leads and conduct research. I also taught myself the useful skill of patience, something I had not practiced well as a reporter. Over the next few years, I would find documents in surprising places. I succeeded in getting people to talk with me years after they first refused. I would also discover it wasn't just the massacre that was largely forgotten, but also the once-substantial presence of the Chinese in the interior of the Pacific Northwest. Nobody had kept their history. The Chinese experience—why they came; what happened to them—became an important part of the story.

I haven't learned everything, but I have learned a great deal. The story that follows is the product of my search. But I must say at the outset that I am grateful for the help of others, most notably Dr. David H. Stratton, a retired professor of history at Washington State University in Pullman, who graciously shared his research, and Priscilla Wegars, volunteer curator of the Asian American Comparative Collection at the University of Idaho, an invaluable adviser on how the Chinese lived and the significance of the little they left behind.

R. Gregory Nokes
January 15, 2009

PART ONE

The Dead

CHAPTER ONE

Tales of Murder

I LISTENED ON a hot July morning in 2003 as a Snake River jetboat captain, idling his boat in front of a cove known as Deep Creek, told two dozen tourists the story, or at least a story, of what happened there in 1887. He said a gang of horse thieves led by an outlaw named Blue Evans had lined up thirty-four Chinese gold miners and shot them one by one after they refused to disclose where they had hidden their gold. Before revving the boat's engines to continue upstream, the captain said it was ironic that the first Chinese killed was the only one who knew English, and the only one who could have revealed the hiding place. For this reason, he told us, the gold was never found.

The captain made no attempt to explain how—since all the miners were killed—anyone could know who did, or did not, speak English, and in what sequence they were murdered. Moreover, the assumption that the gold was never found assumed a great deal, since anyone who found it would surely have done their utmost to keep it a secret.

I saw no point in questioning the captain about the discrepancies in his story. In fact, it was the second version of the massacre I had heard from a river guide. The first time, I dismissed the account as the kind of myth invented by people in the tourism business to entertain their clients. But by now I knew better. While the captain didn't have the details right, he was correct in saying something terrible had happened at Deep Creek to a large group of Chinese miners.

IN THE FALL of 1886, Chea Po would have had no reason to anticipate the terror that lay ahead when his crew of gold miners pushed their boat into the Snake River at Lewiston in the Idaho Territory. They were headed south toward Hells Canyon, a remote chasm of twisting basalt cliffs, known at the time as the Snake River Canyon.[1] Possibly they felt excited at the prospect of finding gold, maybe enough to return to China to their families, from whom they probably had been separated for years. Another crew led by Lee She traveled with them in a second boat—both boats loaded with tools and provisions. The crews pushed them with poles, or pulled them with ropes from shore, through the strong current.

As crew leaders, Chea and Lee were no doubt experienced miners with some knowledge of the canyon, where Chinese had mined since the 1860s. Chea may even have known his destination, a bowl-shaped cove, sixty-five miles south of Lewiston. Here, a stream called Dead Line Creek, now named Deep Creek, flowed out of the Oregon cliffs and across a wide gravel bar into the Snake. The cove was spacious enough for a large camp from which the miners could work the river banks in both directions. On a hillside back from the river was a rock shelter, used previously by Native Americans, which the miners might use for a dwelling or for storage.

The Snake River flows north through Hells Canyon, so the journey against the fast-flowing current must have taken several weeks at least, depending on how frequently the crews stopped to mine. And they probably stopped often, probing the river banks and gravel bars for signs of gold, using pans, rockers, or sluices, all techniques of placer mining—the use of water to wash the ore from dirt and gravel in gold-bearing deposits along streambeds. According to an early settler's account, the Chinese stopped to mine at least once, at a place known as Summer's Bar, but were chased away by a white miner. Recalled one early settler: "Frank Summers was already panning for gold dust on this bar and he resented the Chinamen working on his claim and late in the fall he got after them and made them move."[2]

The Snake River would have been relatively placid for the first thirty miles or so until the Chinese reached the canyon mouth near the Oregon border. But once they were inside the canyon, the deepest in North America, their journey became back breaking and dangerous. Frequently unable to see more than a quarter-mile ahead amid twisting cliffs looming above them like prison walls, the crews faced new obstacles around each bend. Where cliffs rose vertically on both sides of the river, footing was precarious. There were few ways out—they could go forward, or back.

Weather in the canyon is fickle in the early fall. In the mornings, the miners probably wore quilted tunics against the cold wind blowing in their faces, then may have stripped to their waists in the afternoons when temperatures might soar into the eighties. Most would have shielded their heads against the intense sun with wide-brimmed hats of woven bamboo, known to Americans as coolie hats, although the miners weren't coolies—

A view near the mouth of Hells Canyon, the deepest canyon in North America, with forty miles of cliffs more than a mile high. The Chinese miners used poles and ropes from shore to manueuver their boats upstream on the Snake River for sixty-five miles from Lewiston in the Idaho Territory to Deep Creek. (Photo by the author)

they were independent laborers, working for a Chinese employer. Like most Chinese, they probably wore their hair in queues, hung loosely down their backs or wound around their heads, out of their way while they worked.

The miners used flat-bottomed boats, called *bateaus*, capable of maneuvering over river shallows. They would have had to unload their boats to portage around major rapids, such as those now called Wild Goose and Mountain Sheep. The challenge in maneuvering through the rapids was underscored in 1903 when a 125-foot steamer, the *Imnaha*, loaded with equipment for a copper mine, sank after becoming disabled in the Mountain Sheep Rapid.[3] Always, the Chinese faced the threat that the current might tear the boats from their grasp and carry them careening downriver with the loss of their provisions and equipment.

Although the trip must have been physically exhausting, I find it comforting to think the miners might sometimes have paused to admire the beauty of the basalt cliffs, glowing in gold, ochre, and orange in the sunlight, and brooding in blue and ink-dark purple in the shadows. In the evenings, after the sun crossed over the canyon's western rim, they might have been amazed to still see brilliant blue sky overhead, while scarcely able to recognize one another in the dark of the canyon floor. They surely felt the chill breeze that blows after sunset even in midsummer. And they might, after a hard day on the river, have appreciated the quiet of the night, soothed to sleep on the occasional sandy beach by the symphony of the river current. Perhaps, too, they saw a bald eagle circling high above the canyon, with outspread wings rising and falling on the wind currents, or several bighorn sheep looking down from a foothold on a cliff so steep they couldn't imagine how they got there or why they didn't fall. The miners may even have stopped to catch and make a meal of the once-abundant yard-long sockeye salmon, or a ten-foot sturgeon.

Of course, the Chinese might have been too exhausted to experience any of the canyon's majesty, wanting only to collapse at the end of the day on their straw sleeping mats, desperate to rest aching backs and raw and blistered hands. They may have dreamt of the riches they hoped to extract from *Gum San*, their word for Gold Mountain, the name the first immigrants had optimistically given the foreign land.

The crews of Chea Po and Lee She would have traveled the canyon mostly alone and unseen, except by an occasional homesteader or rancher—or the rustlers who preyed on the ranchers. Their journey took them past three large rivers which drain into the Snake: first, the Grande Ronde from the

Deep Creek at the site of the Chinese camp flows out of cliffs on the Oregon side of Hells Canyon and across a gravel bar into the Snake River. The Chinese victims of the massacre mined on the gravel bar and may have been working when they were ambushed. (Photo by the author)

A five-acre site at Deep Creek has been officially named Chinese Massacre Cove to honor those killed there in 1887. The site extends from a boulder-strewn beach upstream to this sandy beach downstream. Deep Creek bisects the site. (Photo by the author)

west, marking the approximate border between Washington and Oregon; then the Salmon from Idaho; and finally the Imnaha, flowing out of the rugged granite peaks of northeastern Oregon's Wallowa Mountains.

Four miles south of the Imnaha, the miners passed Dug Bar, no doubt unaware of its place in history as the crossing point where ten years earlier the legendary Chief Joseph led his band of several hundred Nez Perce in a perilous river crossing after being forced to surrender their northeastern Oregon homeland to white settlers.

WHILE CHEA PO made his camp at Deep Creek about three miles south of Dug Bar, the crew led by Lee She continued another twenty miles upstream to a site known as Salt Creek, where they mined separately from Chea's men at what would prove to be a safe distance from the attack.

According to a 1961 magazine article written by a former Forest Service employee, the late Gerald J. Tucker, Chea's crew uncovered a rich deposit of nuggets and heavy gold flakes along the river bank.[4] Tucker speculated that, centuries earlier, the river had cut through a vein of gold-bearing quartz somewhere upstream and that the gold had lodged in the crevices of the bedrock where the miners found it. He didn't say how he knew all this. But, if he was right, the Chinese scored a major strike, yielding more than the typical find of tiny particles, called flour gold. It would explain why the Chinese mined in the cove for the next eight months. However much they did find, it cost them their lives.

CHAPTER TWO

"Adventurous Boys"

ONE QUESTION I sought to answer at the outset was why the gang killed Chea and the other Chinese. Couldn't they simply have taken their gold and let them be? Who would the Chinese have complained to? The nearest Oregon town, tiny Imnaha, was outside the canyon, thirty miles away over difficult terrain. A larger town, Joseph, was fifty miles distant in the Wallowa Valley. It is doubtful the Chinese, who entered the canyon from Idaho, even knew these towns existed.

If robbed, but otherwise left alone, the Chinese might simply have shrugged off the loss and resumed mining. Or they could have returned the sixty-five miles to Lewiston to report the crime. And what then? Who would have listened, or cared?

BRUCE "BLUE" EVANS led a gang of rustlers who stole cattle and horses on the Oregon side of the Snake River, burned on new brands, and took them across the Snake River into the Idaho Territory to sell. I can only wonder what ran through Evans' mind when he spotted the Chinese mining near the river crossing used by the gang. Did the idea of robbing and killing the miners occur to him at once, or did it develop over time as a way out of his other troubles?

By most accounts a forceful and imposing presence, Evans had gathered around him an improbable gang of schoolboys and small-time ranchers. He was thirty-two at the time of the massacre, and, like some of the others in the gang, led an outwardly respectable life. He had a wife and two children. Why he was called Blue isn't known; possibly it was because he wore a heavy black beard that reflected a bluish cast in the sunlight.

Members of the gang lived on small ranches around the tiny community of Imnaha in what is known as the Wallowa country, now Wallowa County, a remarkably beautiful and rugged area of 3,152 square miles in extreme northeastern Oregon.

NATURAL BARRIERS ISOLATE Wallowa County geographically, even from the rest of Oregon. Three deep gorges form a kind of three-sided moat, with Hells Canyon on the east, the Grande Ronde on the north, and the Minam on the west. Completing the encirclement to the south are the Wallowa Mountains, a range of Alps-like granite peaks, many snow-capped year-round.

Confined within these natural barriers are two fertile valleys, the forty-mile-long Wallowa Valley and, to the east, the smaller Imnaha River Valley. Although the climate and well-watered soils of these two valleys make them ideal for farming and ranching, they were virtually unknown to the outside world until the late 1800s.

Partly because of the region's isolation, settlement came late to the area. When the first ranchers ventured into the Wallowa Valley through the Minam Gorge in 1871, Oregon had already been a state for twelve years, the Civil War was over, and President Abraham Lincoln had been assassinated. An even more important reason than isolation for the late settlement was that the region had been the homeland for the Wallowa band of Nez Perce for thousands of years—the Nez Perce claim was affirmed by an 1855 treaty. But in 1877, following conflicts with settlers who entered the valley under the cover of a fraudulent new 1863 treaty, the Nez Perce were forced to leave.

Notes from a preliminary government survey of the Wallowa Valley, conducted in the fall of 1866, had pointed to the inevitable outcome.

> *Here I found many Indians camped on the banks of the streams, taking great quantities of fish, while their large herds of horses quietly grazed upon luxuriant grass. This valley should be surveyed as soon as practicable, for the wigwam of the savage, will soon give way to the [whites]. Instead of the hunting and fishing grounds of the red men, the valley will teem with a thriving and busy population.*[1]

And so it would be. The region attracted two classes of settlers. Most were hard-working farmers, ranchers, and Civil War veterans, intent on providing a decent life for their families. Many had come west along the Oregon Trail, settled elsewhere, failed to establish themselves, and sought a new opportunity in the fertile valleys in northeastern Oregon. A second and smaller group was of questionable pedigree, interested chiefly in making a fast buck with a minimum of effort. Among these were outlaws, who found the isolated valleys and remote canyons, especially Hells Canyon, ideal for rustling and other criminal pursuits. But both groups had one thing in common: the region offered them a chance, for some a last chance, to make good in the American West.

Evans drew from both groups. The other members of his gang, those who, with Evans, would be charged with the murder of the Chinese, were J. Titus Canfield, Hezekiah "Carl" Hughes, Hiram Maynard, Omar LaRue, and Robert McMillan.[2] A seventh member of the gang, Frank Vaughan, turned state's evidence against the others.

Like most residents in the Wallowa country over the age of ten, members of the Evans gang originated elsewhere. Evans came from the town of Clay in Marshall County, West Virginia, the fourth of nine children in a farming family. He arrived in the Wallowa country in 1879, traveling on the Oregon Trail with Tom Hughes, the wagon master for a train of wagons from Wyoming. In 1881, Evans married Hughes' daughter, Josephine, known as Josie, just age fifteen. The couple homesteaded on Pine Creek, near the former Nez Perce encampment of Chemnisius, a prime grazing area north of the Wallowa Valley, a location offering convenient access into the Imnaha River Valley to the east.[3]

Evans ran his own herd of horses. But he also had an arrangement with another rancher, Fred Nodine, to graze a thousand of his horses, which Evans combined with his own herd. Ranchers such as Nodine sold horses to the Army at nearby Fort Walla Walla, in the Washington Territory, and other posts. Horses also were in demand to manage the expanding herds of cattle being fattened in Montana and Wyoming for Midwest stockyards. Nodine's horses became a source of supply for Evans' own herd. According to an informal history of Wallowa County, written by an early settler, J. Harland "Harley" Horner, Evans' gang stole about one hundred and fifty of Nodine's horses, changing the brand from "a running N to a bar OK."[4] Nodine would later file court complaints listing the value of one of his stolen horses at fifty dollars, and another at thirty-five dollars.[5]

Evans already may have been involved in one murder prior to the massacre. The victim was a rancher-outlaw, Thomas J. Douglas, who gave Dead Line Creek its early name. According to Horner's history, Douglas years earlier had robbed a stagecoach in Montana. There was a shoot-out;

his partner was killed and the stage messenger wounded. Douglas escaped with the iron strongbox containing three gold ingots, which Horner estimated were collectively worth as much as seventy-five thousand dollars, a possibly exaggerated sum, considering the official price of gold was then sixteen dollars an ounce. Following the robbery, Douglas fled to Oregon and hid out near what would become known as the Dug Bar crossing, where he ran some cattle on the nearby bench.[6]

Horner said Douglas, described as balding and middle-aged, hesitated to sell the gold bars because they carried a U.S. government stamp, making them easy to trace. Douglas buried the strongbox near his cabin, occasionally digging up an ingot to file off gold dust to buy his provisions.

There are different versions of the details of Douglas' murder. Horner wrote that gang member Titus Canfield, who occasionally worked for Douglas, observed him filing one of his ingots and shared this information with Evans. A version by another settler, Ross Findley, who wrote his own history of Wallowa County, is that Canfield befriended Douglas, who, in friendship or stupidity, confided his secret.[7] Whichever version is correct, there is agreement that Canfield, either acting alone or with Evans, shot and killed Douglas in December of 1883. The decomposed body was found in the canyon a year later with two bullet holes in its back, Douglas' dead horse nearby. Horner wrote that Evans and Canfield dug up the strongbox and buried it elsewhere.[8]

Not everything written about Evans was negative. Findley reported that Evans once saved the life of a neighboring rancher, John McCaw. According to this account, Evans, while on his way to visit McCaw one evening, encountered a band of rustlers intent on killing McCaw, who happened to be sitting by an open window.

Evans was not close enough to them to recognize any of them, but he realized what had been about to take place. He came on down to McCaw's cabin and told him that he was a fool to sit by an open window the way he was doing where he would be a perfect target for an assassin's bullet.[9]

Findley wrote that the rustlers wanted McCaw out of the way because he somehow impeded their smuggling route into Idaho. Curiously, Findley suggested that the gang that plotted to kill McCaw was the same gang, headed by Evans, that stole Nodine's cattle and would later kill the Chinese. If so, perhaps Evans knew of the McCaw ambush, but, for whatever reason—possibly to curry favor with McCaw—decided to expose it. Or maybe the entire incident was a ruse concocted by Evans. Or, Findley didn't get the story right.

Canfield, twenty-one at the time of the massacre, was Evans' chief sidekick. Born in Steuben County, Indiana, in 1866, he was described in several accounts as a hard-riding, hard-drinking, risk-taking cowboy with bright red hair. He came from a well-known and restless family. His father, Hiram Canfield, and mother, Mary, were among the earliest settlers in the Wallowa country, moving from the Idaho Territory with their four children in 1878. According to Horner, Hiram Canfield was quick to put his own interests ahead of his neighbors'. He first settled in the western Wallowa Valley on property used by a squatter who was away on a trip, and who apparently hadn't been on the property long enough to justify a claim to it. When the squatter returned, he found the Canfields living in his cabin and refusing to move.[10] Not long after, however, the Canfields moved to the upper Wallowa Valley and settled on Pine Creek near Evans, with McCaw's place between them. Titus Canfield was the youngest of four children. He was known by various nicknames: J. T., Tighty, Tight, and Tite. Court records usually refer to him as J. T.

Frank Vaughan, who played a prominent role in the investigation into the murders, was born in Wisconsin and was twenty-one or twenty-two at the time of the crime. Horner put his age at eighteen. However, the 1880 U.S. Census listed the year of his birth as 1865, making him at least twenty-one. The Vaughan family settled along the Imnaha River in 1884 after moving from Nebraska and stopping briefly at Pendleton, Oregon. The large family included Frank Vaughan's mother, Roxie; stepfather, Enoch Vaughan; and uncle, Benjamin Vaughan. Also in the party were Harry Vaughan and his sister, Cora, orphaned cousins of Frank, and their foster parents, the Joseph Smiths.[11] It didn't take long for the family to gain positions of prominence. Horner said Benjamin Vaughan, Frank's uncle, became an osteopath and, as such, the area's first doctor, and also was elected in 1888 as a precinct judge for the Imnaha district. The Vaughans allowed their property be used for the first Imnaha school in 1884, which was replaced a few years later by a new school on property belonging to the family of Ross Findley. Cora Vaughan was the first school teacher, and later became a deputy county clerk.

Somehow, Frank so fooled everyone into believing he was a responsible member of the community that Justice of the Peace J. J. Stanley appointed him a special constable to serve Evans with a subpoena. This was on May 11, 1887—less than three weeks before the massacre. The subpoena ordered Evans to testify in a rustling case against Canfield. Not surprisingly, Vaughan reported back he couldn't find Evans, while claiming expenses for his search. He was reimbursed five dollars for his one hundred miles of riding. Horner suggested he may have camped with Evans at his hideout before reporting back.[12]

The youngest member of the gang was Robert McMillan, the son of Hugh McMillan, a blacksmith who brought his family to the Imnaha Valley in 1886, in search of work. The family lived on a rented property, called Mackies, which became a gang hangout.[13] In a court deposition, McMillan gave his age as fifteen at the time of the murders.[14]

Hezekiah Hughes, also known as "Carl," was born in Kentucky in 1850, making him thirty-seven at the time of the massacre. He was one of nine children of Tom Hughes; his sister, Josephine, married Evans. Hezekiah apparently grazed his own herd of cattle along the Imnaha River.[15]

Hiram Maynard was thirty-eight, the eldest gang member.[16] He also homesteaded on Pine Creek, near Evans, and worked for him at least part-time. Like the others, he may also have operated his own small ranch.

Omar LaRue, probably in his late teens or early twenties, was among the early arrivals on the Imnaha. According to Horner, he was raised by Benjamin Vaughan, Frank's uncle, and, like Canfield, had a reputation as a "good rider and roper."[17]

An eighth member of the gang, Andy Beckelheimer, worked for Fred Nodine, while allegedly helping the gang steal Nodine's horses. He was the only identified gang member not implicated in the massacre.[18]

THE GANG'S HORSE-THIEVING and cattle-rustling activities escaped detection for more than a year. But by early May of 1887, Blue Evans must have felt its rustling days were numbered. Nodine had caught Canfield with six of his horses displaying freshly altered brands, and swore out a warrant, leading to Canfield's arrest on May 10, two weeks before the massacre. Evans, along with Canfield's mother, Mary, posted the eight hundred dollars bond to free Canfield from jail. But if Canfield's arrest wasn't warning enough, Vaughan's appearance at Evans' hideout the next day—with a subpoena ordering him to a court hearing for Canfield—certainly was. Evans logically would have concluded his own role as a rustler was about to be exposed. He also knew horse thieves were dealt with harshly: one suspected rustler, John Hawk, had been shot dead by vigilantes in 1881—with some believing Vaughan's future father-in-law, Sam Adams, had led the vigilantes to Hawk.[19] Evans may have seen the Chinese gold as his ticket out of the county.

Findley suggested in his account it was Canfield who helped recruit fellow students at the Imnaha school to rob and kill the Chinese:

The young outlaw who was attending the school at Imnaha knew all about the movements of the Chinese, and as they had been panning for gold for over six months, he anticipated that they would have about $5,000 in dust panned out. So he proposed to his classmates that they do their country a favor and go down and kill off this band of Chinese miners and get their gold for their trouble.[20]

Findley didn't name the young outlaw, mentioning him only as "a twenty-one-year-old black sheep," but he unquestionably was referring to Canfield, who was twenty-one and a student at the school. Vaughan, McMillan, and LaRue also attended the one-room school, which enrolled thirty students ranging in age from seven to twenty-three for a school term of about three months.[21] As the closest gang member to Evans, Canfield may have been carrying out Evans' instructions. Findley wrote:

[H]e was at heart a criminal. Greed and lust for the goods of others had warped and twisted his mind and soul. His hands had already been stained with the blood of a fellow man, and he naturally became a leader among the older boys.[22]

Why "naturally," Findley didn't say.

THE FIRST FEW times I read Findley's account, I completely overlooked the order in which he listed the motives for the massacre. I had always assumed that stealing the gold was the chief motive. But on a later reading it hit me—Findley was saying that the gang's primary motive was to kill the Chinese. The gold, almost as an afterthought, would be the killers' reward. If he was correct, I had the tragic answer to my question. Robbery wasn't enough—the murders were a savage act of racial hatred.

I initially overlooked this because my attention had already jumped ahead in Findley's account to something equally sinister—the students' reaction to Canfield's "proposal."

> *To induce them to join with him, he even offered to let them have a cut of the Douglas gold. Four of the boys being of an adventurous type agreed to go in with him.*[23]

Adventurous types! I found it difficult to believe anyone could describe the killers simply as boys bent on adventure. Maybe because Findley knew some of the gang—and even in later years counted one, Frank Vaughan, as a good friend—he couldn't bring himself to denounce them as cold-blooded killers.

Findley reported that not all the schoolboys agreed to go along, and "one of the fellows who had been raised in a Christian home refused." Those who did join in agreed to kill anyone who told on them, a threat that extended to the student who refused.[24] I wondered as I read this whether Findley himself was the student from a "Christian home." However, he was only nine years old at the time, and I couldn't imagine the gang would have wanted to include him.

I also wondered how Findley could claim to know the plot in such intimate detail, notwithstanding he was in an ideal position to pick up schoolyard gossip. His father, Alexander Findley, had helped build the school on Findley land in 1886 to replace the earlier school on the Vaughan property, and the teacher in the new school, Cora Samms, lived for a time in the Findley home. I would discover in a later rereading of Findley's account the probable answer. In any event, Findley said it was Canfield who convinced Evans—again neither man was named—to carry out the attack on the Chinese: "The young outlaw then persuaded the leader and one other member of the cattle rustlers band to join them, making seven altogether who were plotting to go down and murder the Chinese miners."[25]

Horner, then seventeen and also a student at the school, wrote in his history that the behavior of the students who belonged to the Evans gang portended trouble, citing their attitude toward their teacher, Cora Samms. They mocked her practice of beginning each school day with a Bible reading and a prayer.

> *Three of the visitors would come in talking very loud with their chapps [sic] ... and spurs on, rattling on the floor and did not remove their hats. These three were the ones mixed up in the China killing on Snake River and other law violations in the valley and tried to act tough. And [sic] was heard later making fun and remarks about her reading from the Bible and having prayer before opening school.*[26]

Another troublemaker was "a nice-looking young lady" who would eventually be expelled without showing the slightest regret: "As she went out the door, laughing, she yelled back, saying, 'Good-bye, all'." This same student, Horner wrote, later married one of the gang members. He may have been writing about Minnie Adams, who would marry Frank Vaughan in 1890, three years after the massacre.

CHAPTER THREE

Miles from Punyu

THE FIRST BODY was discovered floating in the Snake River near Lime Kiln, about thirty miles south of Lewiston. Flushed from Hells Canyon by heavy spring rains and snowmelt, the badly decomposed body had been in the water for weeks.

Another body surfaced a day or so later at Penewawa Bar in the Washington Territory, forty miles downriver from Lewiston. A third appeared at Log Cabin Bar, also in Washington. Over the next few days, four more bodies floated mysteriously out of Hells Canyon. Meanwhile, a boatload of Chinese emerged from the canyon with the first account of what had happened. The details were reported in *The Lewiston Teller,* a now defunct weekly, on June 16, 1887:

> *A boatload of Chinamen came down the Snake River on Saturday last and brought the news that another boatload of Chinese had been murdered about one hundred and fifty miles [sic] above here by some unknown parties. They claim that the Chinamen, ten in number, who were murdered, had upwards of three thousand dollars on them, having been mining on the river for the past year. They found their boat with blankets and provisions in, and but three of the Chinamen have been found, and these in the river, two of whom were shot and the third could not be captured. Some think the Chinamen murdered them, while others think Indians or whites, but the mystery may never be solved.[1]*

A second article two weeks later provided additional detail, including attempts to retrieve the bodies.

> *J. K. Vincent and a Chinese merchant left here on Monday last in a small boat for Riparia to procure the bodies of the Chinamen that were found in the river. They succeeded in getting one of the bodies which they brought up on Thursday's boat, and the same was buried in the Chinese cemetery near this city. We are informed that the body was brutally mangled, having two gunshot wounds in the back, one arm partly cut off, and the head nearly severed from the body. Other bodies were seen in the drift, but will be unable to be taken out until the water goes down.[2]*

OVER TIME, ESTIMATES of the number of dead would rise to thirty-four, although the precise number was never officially declared or documented. Correspondence from the Chinese government, now on file in the National Archives, provided sketchy information for ten of the victims, those with the surnames Chea and Kong. All were from Punyu, part of the city of Guangzhou (then Canton) in southeastern China's Guangdong Province (then Kwangtung), the home province for a majority of the Chinese immigrants.[3]

The ten, including crew leader Chea Po, were organized by—and possibly worked for—the Sam Yup Company, one of the Chinese Six Companies, headquartered in San Francisco. The Chinese Six Companies combined the functions of employer, labor union, and fraternal order, and managed diplomatic relations prior to the establishment of formal relations between the United States and China in 1878. It also maintained a registry of Chinese immigrants, with each company representing workers from specific districts in China.[4] The Chinese Six Companies is better known today by its official name, the Chinese Consolidated Benevolent Association; it is headquartered in San Francisco with branches in major American cities, including Portland. The Sam Yup Company, literally "three districts," represented workers from the Shuntak, Punyu, and Namhoi districts, the latter two part of the port city of Guangzhou.

Certain assumptions can be made about the victims. The eight with the surname Chea would have been members of a single clan—Chinese with the same name frequently worked together.[5] They would have been in the United States at least five years, arriving prior to the enactment of the onerous Chinese Exclusion Act in 1882, which closed the nation's

A Chinese mining with a rocker, also called a cradle, with shovel and pails of rocks and gravel, somewhere in California. (Bancroft Library, University of California, Berkeley)

doors to additional Chinese laborers. They had likely borrowed money—approximately forty dollars—from a hiring agent to pay for their passage on a steamship in Hong Kong, arriving weeks later in San Francisco or Portland, the two major West Coast ports of disembarkation for Chinese immigrants. The money would be deducted later from their wages, a process known as the credit-ticket system. Like most Chinese laborers, they would have come alone, leaving families behind.

Perhaps Chea Po and his clansmen were among the 1,272 Chinese laborers who arrived in San Francisco in 1869 aboard the steamer *Great Republic*, the arrival recorded at the Pacific Mail Steamship Company wharf by an unknown writer for the *Atlantic Monthly* magazine.

> *A living stream of the blue-coated men of Asia, bearing long bamboo poles across their shoulders, from which depended packages of bedding matting, clothing, and things of which we know neither the names nor the uses, pours down the plank, the moment that the word is given, "All ready!" They appear to be of an average age of twenty-five years—very few being under fifteen, and none apparently over forty years—and though somewhat less in stature than Caucasians, healthy, active, and able-bodied to a man. As they come down upon the wharf, they separate into messes or gangs of ten, twenty, or thirty each, being recognized through some to us incomprehensible free-masonry system of signs by the agents of the Six Companies as they come, are assigned places on the long, broad-shedded wharf, which has been cleared especially for their accommodation and the convenience of the customs officers ...*
>
> *They are all dressed in coarse but clean and new blue cotton blouses and loose baggy breeches, blue cotton cloth stockings which reach to the knee, and slippers or shoes, with heavy wooden soles (these they will discard for American boots, when they go up country to work in the dust and mud); and most of them carry one or two broad-brimmed hats of split bamboo and huge palm leaf fans to shield them from the burning sun in the mountains of California.*[6]

Or they may have come directly to Portland on the *Belle of Oregon*, a three-masted bark launched in 1876 at Bath, Maine, and built expressly to transport wheat from Portland to China, and return with Chinese laborers.

The ship transported at least two loads of laborers from Hong Kong to Portland, and one to San Francisco.[7]

Immigration directly from Hong Kong to Portland was in full swing by 1868 to meet a demand for railroad workers. In 1882, the last year of unrestricted immigration, five thousand Chinese arrived in Portland by ship.[8]

At whichever port they disembarked, a Sam Yup Company agent likely would have met Chea Po and the other men from Punyu to arrange employment on the railroads or in other endeavors. (He also would help arrange for their bodies to be returned to China, in the event they died on American soil.[9]) An agent, or broker, typically a Chinese, would negotiate the terms of their employment, collect their pay, and deduct repayment of the money borrowed for their tickets.

If Chea's crew landed at San Francisco, they might have continued to Portland by coastal steamer. Or they might have worked their way north overland from San Francisco, mining on the American, Feather, or Trinity rivers in California before crossing into southern Oregon where gold had been discovered in the Rogue and Umpqua valleys in 1852. By 1858, more than one thousand Chinese were mining in southern Oregon. When gold was discovered in northern Idaho in the early sixties, they might have relocated once again,[10] perhaps walking the entire distance.

The possibility I favor is that Chea and his crew disembarked in Portland and were among the thousands of Chinese recruited to clear land, grade track beds, and lay rails for the new railroads spreading across the Pacific Northwest in the 1870s and 1880s—although in some cases laying track was reserved for Caucasians.[11]

To continue this not improbable line of speculation ... When the railroad was completed, they would have been laid off together with thousands of other workers, Chinese and Caucasian, and left adrift to survive as they might in an alien land. They may have turned to mining as one of the few work opportunities available to them. But for whatever reason, and whichever path they took, they ended up in Lewiston, as had many other Chinese before them. The same scenario might apply to Lee She and members of his crew.

LEWISTON TODAY IS a modern city with a population of 30,904 in the 2000 Census. Downstream dams have widened, deepened, and slowed the Snake River, transforming the city into an inland port from where barges carry the region's wheat and other goods to ocean-going ships in Portland, three hundred and fifty miles to the southwest. But when Chea Po and Lee She set out with their crews in the fall of 1886, Lewiston was only just recovering from a long economic downturn, attributed to a near collapse of northern Idaho's gold-mining activity.

The city is named for Meriwether Lewis, who crossed the region with William Clark in 1805 and 1806. It occupies the lower right side of a T formed by the Clearwater River from the east, and the Snake River on the south and west. The rivers combine at Lewiston into a larger Snake that turns sharply west into Washington to merge with the south-flowing Columbia River.

Prior to the discovery of gold nearby, there was no such place as Lewiston. But when gold was found along the Clearwater River in 1860 and 1861—near what is now Pierce, Idaho—it ignited an overnight gold rush, creating the need for a centrally located town to supply the thousands of miners pouring into the region. Thus was born Lewiston, first called Ragtown. Caucasians came first, followed soon after by Chinese. Within a few years, Lewiston claimed a population of several thousand, mostly miners and speculators with a get-rich-quick mentality.[12] When Congress created the new Idaho Territory in 1863, Lewiston was the logical choice for the capital, administering an enormous territory that initially included the Montana and Wyoming territories.

By mid-decade, however, the boom had run its course. Caucasian miners had scooped up most of the easily mined gold from claims along the Clearwater and its tributaries, then departed in droves for new and more promising gold strikes in southern Idaho. With nothing but mining to sustain its economy, Lewiston's population plummeted to just 359 in 1864.[13] Adding insult to injury, the city lost its status as territorial capital to upstart Boise in 1865, a major civic humiliation.

But just as the boom didn't last, neither did the bust. By the 1880s, the population was growing again, with a Census count of 782, including sixty-two Chinese. Wheat, growing in great abundance on the surrounding plateau, had emerged as the new gold for the Caucasian population. Hundreds more Chinese lived in nearby mining towns and camps, dominating what remained of the region's mining industry.

WHEN THE CHINESE first arrived, white miners viewed them as unwanted intruders. Even the possibility of Chinese competition alarmed Caucasians. To keep the gold for themselves, the miners organized whites-only mining districts. Typical was an edict from the Oro Fino mining district on April 14, 1861, which affirmed "the complete exclusion of the Chinese and Asiatic races and the South Pacific Ocean Islanders from the mines."[14] Similar bans were enacted by miners in the nearby Warren, Nez Perce, and Salmon River mining districts.[15]

Chinese didn't arrive in Lewiston in appreciable numbers until 1865, although a few may have come as early as 1861.[16] While barred from mining, they took whatever other jobs were available—washing laundry, carrying supplies, and digging the ditches that brought water to the mining camps from often distant streams. The Chinese knew from their earlier experiences in California that after impatient Caucasians had mined the most accessible gold, they would be only too happy to sell their claims to the Chinese, or simply abandon them.[17]

That is indeed what happened. Once Chinese could move into the mining camps and work the old claims, they soon outnumbered Caucasians in mining towns throughout the region. Oro Fino, for example, counted 550 Chinese to just 120 Caucasians in 1866. Nearly six of every ten miners in the Idaho Territory were Chinese in 1870—3,853 Chinese out of 6,579 miners. It was the same in Oregon—2,428 Chinese out of 3,965 miners.[18] Chinese also ran many of the pack teams carrying supplies from Lewiston to mountain mining camps.

The Sam Yup Company, as an employer, typically bought up old claims and provided the tools and provisions for the Chinese miners. In return, it took possession of the gold from which wages were paid.[19]

CHAPTER FOUR

Why They Came

THE CHINESE LABORERS who emigrated to the American West during the latter half of the nineteenth century came for the reason other immigrants come, to find work. But there was one significant difference: most had no interest in remaining in the United States or assimilating into American culture. Mostly men, they came to earn enough money to support their families, mired in grinding poverty back home. They didn't require much, maybe a few hundred dollars, to retire in their home villages.[1]

Largely keeping to themselves, Chinese men lived in clusters of ramshackle dwellings on the fringes of the white community's cities and towns—clusters that became Chinatowns. Here, many sought whenever possible to maintain the customs of their home villages, wearing the same clothes, eating the same food, winding their hair in queues, with little opportunity to learn English—and quite possibly little interest.[2]

They came in two great waves, the first during the 1850s and 1860s in search of gold, following the discoveries at Sutter's Mill in California in 1848. Tens of thousands more immigrated during the 1860s and 1870s to help build the railroads. Chinese also cleared land, drained swamps, dug ditches, fished, worked in salmon canneries, farmed, made cigars, and ran laundries, called washhouses.

As noted earlier, Chinese-American historians estimate that about three hundred thousand Chinese emigrated to the United States and its mainland territories during the latter half of the nineteenth century. This figure takes into account the two-way flow of immigrants, including those who returned to China.

The largest number of Chinese in the U.S. at one time in this period was an unofficial 132,300 in 1882, before immigration restrictions took effect.[3] Fully two-thirds were engaged in mining or worked on railroads.[4] The official population of Chinese in the U.S. in the 1880 Census was 105,465. Of these, California had the largest number (75,132), followed by Oregon (9,510), Idaho (3,379), and Washington (3,186). No Chinese were listed for Wallowa County in 1890, the first Census after the county was established, and just one in 1900.

Table 1. Chinese Population in the United States and Far West

	1860	1870	1880	1890
United States	34,933	63,199	105,465	107,488
California	34,933	49,277	75,132	72,472
Oregon	---	3,330	9,510	9,450
Idaho	---	4,274	3,379	2,007
Washington	---	234	3,186	3,260

Source: U.S. Census

Table 2. Chinese Population in Selected Counties

	1870	1880	1890
OREGON COUNTIES			
Baker	680	787	398
Grant	940	905	326
Jackson	634	337	224
Union	45	235	125
Multnomah	508	1,983	5,184
IDAHO COUNTIES			
Boise	1,754	1,225	421
Idaho	425	738	278
Nez Perce	747	198	55
Owyhee	368	239	214
Shoshone	468	296	201
WASHINGTON COUNTIES			
Jefferson	19	96	43
King	33	246	458
Kitsap	13	149	60
Pierce	7	155	9
Spokane	--	219	361
Wahkiakum	15	559	304
Walla Walla	42	512	351
Whitman	--	530	155

Source: U.S. Census. County figures compiled in Dirlik, *American Frontier*, Appendix, 453-59.

That a majority of the immigrants came from Guangdong Province is partly explained by the history of foreign activity in Guangzhou and Hong Kong, China's major ports for foreign shipping. Exposure to foreigners and their customs contributed to a willingness to risk emigration to a strange land.[5] The people of Guangdong also had a more adventurous background, as the province was settled by people moving south from other regions of China.[6] Significantly, prior to 1840, Guangzhou was the only port trading with the West. This changed after the Opium War when the victorious Western powers forced China to open five ports to shipping and to cede control of Hong Kong to Great Britain.[7]

The Chinese had ample reasons to emigrate.[8] The autocratic rule of the Qing (Manchu) dynasty, in power since the mid-1600s, had been weakened by chaos and rebellion, including the devastating Taiping rebellion of 1850 to 1864, which killed and estimated twenty million to thirty million Chinese.[9] Uprisings, banditry, and famine took their toll in Guangdong.[10] The province was unable to produce enough food to feed its population, estimated at twenty-eight million in 1850—of a total Chinese population of four hundred and thirty million—in an area not a great deal larger than Oregon.[11] Wrote one historian:

> *This domestic turmoil caused great economic dislocations and distress and was one of the important factors forcing so many Chinese to decide to migrate from the Pearl River Delta region. Since the Cantonese had long had maritime contacts, it was only natural that, when the news came of the discovery of gold in California and good wages to be had, some would consider emigration to America as a solution to their economic difficulties.[12]*

The Chinese contribution to the development of the American West was substantial. But their efforts won them scant praise and little recognition—they didn't fit neatly into the popular narrative of the conquest of the West by courageous white pioneers and gun-toting cowboys.

AS WORKERS, THE Chinese proved themselves on the Central Pacific Railroad, the western leg of the first transcontinental railroad, completed in 1869. During the first two years of construction, Caucasian laborers completed only about fifty miles of track. Faced with a shortage of labor, and frustrated by costly delays, the owners turned to Chinese workers, eventually employing as many as eleven thousand.[13] The gamble—and so it was seen at the time—paid off. Chinese workers heroically built a key section of track through California's rugged Sierra Nevada range, working in tunnels under mountain snowdrifts, risking being buried alive, as some were. Others hung from baskets over sheer granite cliffs to drill holes for dynamite, with an occasional luckless man blasted from his perch.[14]

The Chinese were soon in demand on railroads throughout the West. Recruiters in China found the workers. Ships of the two major American steamship lines, the Pacific Mail Steamship Company and the Occidental and Oriental Steamship Company, brought them to American shores. Pacific Mail received a government postal subsidy that assured it of handsome profits.[15] One scholar estimates that steamships carried two hundred thousand Chinese to West Coast ports between 1876 and 1890, and more than half that many back to China, where they visited or remained.[16]

As many as fifteen thousand Chinese worked on the Northern Pacific Railroad during the 1870s and 1880s, laying track in northern Washington, Idaho, and Montana. Chinese also worked in large numbers on the Oregon and California Railroad, connecting San Francisco and Portland, and the Oregon Railway and Navigation Co., helping build the line from Portland to connect with the Northern Pacific at Wallula in Washington. Another six thousand, five hundred workers were employed on the Canadian Pacific.[17]

Leland Stanford, governor of California from 1861 to 1863, and one of the owners of the Central Pacific, praised the Chinese railway workers in a report to President Andrew Johnson on October 10, 1865: "As a class they are quiet, peaceable, patient, industrious and economical. Ready and apt to learn all the different kinds of work required in railroad building, they soon became as efficient as the white laborers."[18]

Within a decade, however, circumstances changed dramatically. Tens of thousands of workers, both Chinese and Caucasian, were laid off during the financial panic of 1873 and the long recession that followed. What had been a labor shortage, turned into a glut, and workers were thrown into a fierce and sometimes violent competition for scarce jobs. Whites were enraged that some employers preferred to hire Chinese, caring more about low wages and work habits than skin color. Chinese also angered whites by refusing to join strikes for higher wages; in some cases, they were employed as strikebreakers. Labor conflict fueled rampant racism, especially in the West. Chinese were despised for their skin color, ridiculed for their customs, and attacked for taking jobs whites felt belonged to them.

Expelled from many small communities, notably in California, but also in the Pacific Northwest, Chinese gravitated to the emerging new Chinatowns in the cities. However, the more they congregated in any one place, the more unwelcome they frequently became.

The loneliness and isolation endured by many laborers is reflected in the following letter to his wife from an unidentified Chinese miner in the John Day area of Oregon. It surely mirrored the feelings of many other Chinese living far from home.

My Beloved Wife:

It has been several autumns now since your dull husband left you for a far remote alien land. Thanks to my hearty body I am all right. Therefore stop embroidering worries about me.

Yesterday I received another of your letters. I could not keep the tears from running down my cheeks when thinking about the miserable and needy circumstances of our home, and thinking back to the time of our separation.

Because of our destitution I went out, trying to make a living. Who could know that the fate is always opposite to man's design? Because I can get no gold, I am detained in this secluded corner of a strange land. Furthermore, my beauty, you are implicated in an endless misfortune. I wish this paper would console you a little. That is all that I can do for now ...[19]

BY THE 1880s Lewiston had an established Chinatown in an area between First and Fourth, and C and D streets,[20] near the mudflats of the Clearwater River. As elsewhere, Chinese were shunted to the least desirable real estate. Impressive Lombardy poplars shaded many of Lewiston's streets, but didn't extend into Chinatown, even though Chinese dug the six-mile irrigation ditch from the Clearwater to water the poplars, now long gone.

For the most part, the Chinese in Lewiston lived relatively undisturbed by the white population. But a devastating fire that destroyed much of Chinatown on November 19, 1883, was a reminder that violence lurked just beneath the surface. A 1903 history of North Idaho said the fire was not mourned in the white community "as it removed a block which had been an eyesore in the city for a long time."[21]

While no evidence has survived indicating the fire was anything but an accident—an overturned kerosene lantern was blamed—the shouts and cheers of whites, pleading with firefighters to let Chinatown burn, surely terrified the Chinese. Using a horse-drawn pumper, firefighters ignored the crowd and fought the flames, not so much to save Chinatown, perhaps, but to protect a blacksmith shop owned by Lott Wiggins, a well-known Caucasian. They were too late. Fire destroyed the shop, along with fourteen Chinese dwellings, and, possibly, an early Chinese temple.[22]

AS IN MANY other towns and cities in the West, Lewiston's Chinese built temples to venerate their deities. The last Lewiston temple, constructed in 1890, was located near the corner of Sixth and C streets and was built with contributions from several hundred businesses and individuals, all Chinese. Four wooden donor boards listed contributors' names, with one providing only the first names of six women, leading to conjecture they were prostitutes. The formal name of the temple was Liet Sing Gung, or Palace of Many Gods. But it was popularly known as the Beuk Aie Temple, taking this name from Beuk Aie, God of the North. None of the several deities venerated at the temple had greater importance to Chinese miners than Beuk Aie, the deity for water and flood control.[23]

Unlike temples elsewhere, the temple at Sixth and C did not house images of the gods. The temple was Daoist, embracing multiple deities. The altar was draped in rich brocade embroidered with gold and featured a green plaque that listed in gold lettering the names of five principal deities.[24] Chinese religious beliefs were syncretic, blending features of Buddhism, Confucianism, and Daoism.[25] Chinese visited the temples to worship, honor an ancestor, or simply capture something of the spirit of their native land. Bowing before the altar, they might light a stick of incense or make an offering of fruit or liquor to one of the deities.

The temple also was a place where a Chinese miner might learn his fortune. Perhaps Chea Po had once taken the cup from the altar table and shaken out a numbered stick, whose number corresponded to a numbered fortune in the *I Ching*, or *Book of Changes*. Or he might have dropped two rounded wooden fortune blocks, called the *gau boi*, in front of the altar, asking whether he would ever return home. If both fell face up, his wish might be granted. If face down, denied. If on opposite sides, the outcome was inconclusive.

CHAPTER FIVE

More Tales of Murder

EARLY ON IN my research, I was faced with sorting through a multitude of theories as to how the massacre occurred. Some, such as the scenario advanced by the jetboat captain, I dismissed out of hand. The two accounts that finally emerged as most credible were from the separate histories written by Ross Findley and Harland Horner.

The Findley account is included in a long series of newspaper articles that started in the now-defunct weekly, the *Chief Joseph Herald,* and finished in the *Wallowa County Chieftain,* over a two-year period, from 1957 to 1959. They record the experiences of his father and mother, Alexander and Sarah Jane Findley, who arrived in the Wallowa country in 1872, and settled along the Imnaha River in 1879. Alexander Findley had come West by wagon train from St. Joseph's, Missouri, to first settle in the Willamette Valley in 1848 and later relocate in the Grande Ronde Valley before finally journeying into the Wallowa country—he and his wife were said to be the first settlers to bring a wagon into the valley.[1] A long-time valley resident, the late Grace Bartlett, put me in touch with a descendant of Findley's, who generously let me copy the two hundred and thirty-four pages.

The major shortcoming of Findley's version is that he named no names, most likely because he knew some of the accused, both as a schoolboy and as an adult, and wanted to protect their reputations, such as they were. He wrote that in the years following the massacre he frequently ran cattle with Frank Vaughan and Frank's cousin, Harry, and "became well-acquainted with both of them," recalling "memories of many happy days."[2]

Findley placed the massacre at Chinamen's Gulch, described as "a sheltered cove." A Forest Service map lists a Chinamen's Gulch several miles downstream from Deep Creek, near the confluence of the Snake and Imnaha rivers. No one else has placed the massacre at the gulch, although it is possible some Chinese were killed there. Writing decades after the massacre, Findley may have confused Chinamen's Gulch with Deep Creek, which has a sheltered cove.

Findley said after agreeing to rob and kill the Chinese the gang members reconnoitered along the Imnaha River. Their hideout in Hells Canyon would be a cabin owned by a prominent rancher, George Craig, which had once belonged to the slain rancher-outlaw, Thomas Douglas. Craig's name would later surface in connection with other aspects of the massacre. Findley wrote in his account:

> *The gang met on the Imnaha and rode down to the Snake River on May 25 and watched the Chinese miners from a hillside. They spent the night in George Craig's cabin which Craig used when he was looking after his stock during the winter. The next morning, one stayed at the cabin to prepare breakfast, and the others went down to murder the Chinese miners. They left one to hold the horses and another as a lookout above the camp to warn of anyone coming down the river. Another was sent below the camp to warn of anyone approaching from below. Then the other three took a position on the hillside above the camp and with high-powered rifles began the slaughter of thirty-one innocent and defenseless Chinese whose only weapon of defense was a 22-caliber rifle. The rifles barked and one by one the Chinamen were shot down like sheep killing dogs [sic]. They killed all but one until their ammunition ran out and when he started to flee in a boat, they had to run after him and finish him off with rocks.*[3]

Findley said the killers threw the bodies in the river, running high for that time of year, and burned the tools, tents, and other camp supplies. He added that they took all the gold, except for one bag found years later by stockmen digging a trail round a hillside. "All evidence of any mining operations were covered up. The murderers hid their loot and rode back to the settlement thinking they had committed a perfect crime."[4]

Horner, like Findley, grew up with some of the gang members and knew many as schoolmates. Horner's father, Seymour Horner, brought his family to the Imnaha Valley from Boise, Idaho, in 1884, homesteading near Camp Creek, which flows into Little Sheep Creek a mile south of the town of Imnaha.

Horner's history of Wallowa County, written during the 1930s and 1940s, fills sixteen hundred typewritten pages. Never published, it was privately held until it was turned over to the Oregon Historical Society Research Library, where I read it in its entirety.

Unlike Findley, Horner did name some names, perhaps because he didn't claim the killers as friends. At the time he wrote his account, he was the county historian.

Horner suggested the massacre was a spur-of-the-moment decision, rather than planned in advance. He said the gang attempted to swim a group of stolen horses across the river to Idaho. However, they couldn't get them across, and, after several horses drowned, the rustlers sought to borrow a boat from the Chinese, mining nearby. But the Chinese refused them. It was at that point, Horner wrote, that Evans argued for killing the Chinese.

> So then they discussed what was the best thing to do. And Evans said, "Boys, lets kill the damn Chinamen, throw them in the river and get these horses across." And Canfield said, "Yes. Let's get the damn Chinamen out of the way and get what gold they have." And Evans agreed.[5]

According to Horner's account, the other five were at first reluctant, and the gang returned to the Craig cabin, where Evans and Canfield persuaded them. Hughes would remain at the cabin as a lookout.

> So the six went down where the Chinamen were working, or near. They slipped around close, where they had a good view of them, and began pouring the lead into them, surprising them completely and killing them all. In their sworn evidence, they said there was only ten. But the report at the time was there were 34. They threw all the bodies into the Snake River and one Chinaman not being dead managed to get ashore. And they saw him, and LaRue grabbed up a piece of driftwood and knocked him on the head and kicked him back in the river. The Chinamen had only one small revolver which he emptied at them. One bullet hitting Vaughan in the leg which made him quite lame. And later, when asked what made him limp, he would say his horse fell on him.[6]

Horner located the massacre at Dead Line Creek, now Deep Creek. Depositions discovered in the county safe, given by some of the gang members in 1888, also placed the murders at Dead Line Creek, using the name interchangeably with Deep Creek—leaving no doubt they were the same.[7]

Horner offered other details not found elsewhere. His was the only report to say that the Chinese fought back, and that they shot Vaughan in the leg before being overwhelmed. In a rare instance of attribution, a hand-written notation in the margins of Horner's history said the information on Vaughan's wound came from Harry Vaughan.[8] Horner also wrote of a related killing not mentioned anywhere else. The victim was an orphan boy named Tommy Harmon, whom Evans had taken under his wing, either to raise him, or provide a temporary home. According to Horner, Harmon was with the gang at the Craig cabin, but remained behind when the others went to the Chinese camp. Upon hearing later of the killing, Harmon ran away. Fearing that the boy would talk, Evans "immediately jumped on his horse and went after him. But came back after awhile without him. And when asked about it, said he would tell no tales. It was said, several years later, the skeleton of a boy was found in small cave."[9]

A third account deserving attention was written by Dr. David Stratton, a since-retired professor of history at Washington State University in Pullman. Stratton concluded in a 1983 article that thirty-one miners were killed at two locations in three separate shootings over two days. He wrote that the gang killed the first ten Chinese at Robinson Gulch, a half-mile downstream from Deep Creek. While Stratton's account is partly at odds with more recently uncovered information, it is worth telling because it points up the difficulty of trying to determine what actually did happen. His account reads in part:

On or about May 25, 1887, some or all of the gang formulated a plan to murder the Orientals. While Vaughan stayed behind at the cabin and prepared dinner, the other six rode their horses to the steep slopes overlooking the Snake River. Hughes and Maynard were posted along the river as lookouts, one upstream and the other downstream from the massacre site, while young McMillan was left in charge of the horses. Canfield and LaRue, who stood above on the rim of Robinson Gulch and Evans, who was stationed below, began shooting down at the unsuspecting miners on the gravel bar. As the shots of the long-range rifles echoed up the canyon walls above the roar of the river, the trapped Chinese scrambled helplessly about trying to escape. Despite their best efforts, they were killed one by one, and some were horribly mutilated in the process or soon afterwards.[10]

Looking upstream on the Snake River from Deep Creek. The large boulders would have blocked escape when the Chinese were ambushed at their mining camp. (Photo by the author)

Stratton believed the killers fired until they had exhausted their ammunition and then retired to the cabin for the night. He wrote that Evans, Canfield, and LaRue returned to the river the next day and killed eight more Chinese who happened by the camp. The killers then traveled by boat to a river bar about four miles away where they killed thirteen others, for a total of thirty-one dead. Stratton relied in part on records in the National Archives, along with newspaper clippings, and information developed by Works Progress Administration researchers during the 1930s Depression.

While Stratton did not mention Deep Creek by name, that location fits his description of the location of the killings. The cliffs behind Robinson Gulch slope away from the river at a gradual incline, minimizing the opportunity for ambush, while the cliffs above Deep Creek encircle the cove where the Chinese made camp. Also, when I visited, there was not a gravel bar at Robinson Gulch, while a large bar of rock, gravel, and sand fronts the Deep Creek site. It should be noted, however, that bars are unstable and can be swept way in a river flood, to reform elsewhere.

Stratton's account lacked the benefit of the court records found in the Wallowa County safe, which surfaced after he wrote his article. He also didn't refer to the Horner and Findley accounts.

There are other versions of the massacre, including this one from the *Illustrated History of Union and Wallowa Counties*, published in 1902, which indicated Oregon authorities didn't learn of the crime for nearly a year.

> *In the spring of 1888 it was discovered that the fair fame of Wallowa County had again been stained by a horrible murder. The fall previous,*

thirty-four Chinamen, with full equipment, moved onto one of the bars
on Snake River, just above the point where the Imnaha joins it, and
began mining for gold. It was generally supposed that the Chinese had
considerable gold dust, many thousands of dollars' worth, although
the exact amount of their possession was unknown. After opening of
spring, the attention of a party of men was attracted by the absence
of signs of life around the camp. The men made investigations, which
resulted in the finding of the bodies of two Chinamen, killed by
shooting in the head. The other Orientals were nowhere to be seen.
On the bank near the river several small piles of cartridge shells were
discovered, and other evidences that a battle had taken place were not
lacking. It was said that during the winter several bodies of Chinamen
had been found near Lewiston, indicating that the missing victims had
been set adrift in a scuttled boat or thrown into the river.[11]

All the accounts differ in important respects. Stratton, for example, put
Frank Vaughan at the cabin, playing no active role in the massacre, while
Horner said Vaughan not only was at the massacre site, but was wounded in
the shooting. Horner and Findley disagreed over the location of the shooting
and the number of victims—Horner said thirty-four, Findley thirty-one. But
Horner and Findley sadly mirrored each other in one important respect:
they had few words of sympathy for the Chinese victims.

CHAPTER SIX

The Judge and "The Chinaman"

AMONG THE FIRST to examine the bodies floating out of the mouth of Hells Canyon in June of 1887 was Judge Joseph K. Vincent, who held the dual positions in Lewiston of justice of the peace for Nez Perce County and U.S. commissioner.[1] Letters written by Vincent to the Chinese consulate in San Francisco described the mutilated condition of the slain Chinese. Of the first body, found at Lime Kiln, Vincent wrote:

Description, about 5 feet 6 inches high, 4 very large teeth, 2 above standing out, 2 below standing out and down. He had on clothes, a leather belt around his waist, shot in the back just below right shoulder blade, 2 cuts in back of head, one on each side done with an axe. Found about June 16th.

The second body, recovered at Penewawa Bar, was naked. "No clothes— shot in the breast, just below the heart, head very much cut and chopped."

The third body, pulled from the river at Log Cabin Bar, was in the worst shape of all.

About 5 feet 7 or 8 inches tall, had on clothes and boots. 2 shot wounds in small of back near back bone, head off as though chopped, left arm off between elbow and shoulder, both arm and head in coat which was fastened to his body, held there by belt around his waist; he was lodged in a large drift pile when found. Some recognized him as Ah Yow.

There is no further mention in any of the correspondence or documents of Ah Yow, the first victim identified.

While it is conceivable the river itself had torn apart the bodies, Vincent was convinced the wounds resulted from a savage attack, inflicted by killers driven by intense hatred: "It was the most cold-blooded cowardly treachery, I have ever heard tell of on this coast. And I am a 49er. Every one was shot, cut up and stripped and thrown in the river."[2]

Other bodies were discovered that fall deep in the canyon. The Oregon rancher George Craig and his son, Frazier, found skeletons lodged in rocks and washed up on gravel bars. "The coyotes or buzzards had cleaned most of the flesh off of them, so we did not know they were Chinamen," Craig recalled in a newspaper interview years later. "We couldn't imagine how so many men had been killed without our hearing about it."[3]

Shortly before Vincent wrote to the consulate, an investigator for the Sam Yup Company, Lee Loi, arrived in Lewiston and reportedly offered Vincent one thousand dollars to find the killers.[4] Officials at the San Francisco-based company had read newspaper accounts of the massacre and turned to Vincent for help, probably because of his title as a U.S. commissioner. However, Vincent may not have been an ideal choice. He was sixty-five, well past the age at which most men would undertake such an arduous and potentially dangerous mission.

MORE IS KNOWN about Vincent than anyone else involved with the massacre. He had already led a life filled with more adventure, and misadventure, than any ten men his age. He also had established himself as something of an opportunist, even a hustler, interested in making a fast buck without a great deal of effort.

Vincent was born in Salem, Massachusetts, on June 26, 1822. He left home in his teens to become a sailor, following in the footsteps of his seaman father, also named Joseph, said to have been murdered either in the West Indies or the Sandwich Islands (Hawaii). After crewing on ships in the Pacific for a dozen years, Vincent left the sea in 1851 to join the California gold rush, presumably jumping ship in San Francisco, as did hundreds of other seamen. He tried mining along the Feather River, apparently without a great deal of success, as he next turned up as a gold miner in southern Oregon's Rogue River country.[5] The 1860 Census had him living in Josephine County.

In Oregon, Vincent volunteered to fight in a brutal war against the Rogue River Indians that erupted in 1854, ignited by conflict between the miners and the tribe. One account, written in 1903 while Vincent was still alive, said the tribe held him captive for five days, during which he suffered serious frostbite to his feet and legs before being rescued.[6] The injuries apparently weren't debilitating, however, as Vincent subsequently led a long life in apparent good physical health.

After the outbreak of the Civil War, Vincent enlisted in the Army in 1862 at Fort Walla Walla in the Washington Territory. He served in the West, assigned to Fort Lapwai, east of Lewiston, to keep watch over the new Nez Perce reservation at Lapwai. The reservation had been established by the same 1863 treaty that defrauded the Wallowa band of the Nez Perce of their homeland in the Wallowa country.

Departing the Army in 1865, Vincent settled in Lewiston, where he ran a tavern. That same year, he was appointed sheriff of Nez Perce County after the newly elected sheriff, James Fisk, was unable to post the necessary bond. Vincent served only until the next election—there is no record of his seeking election. He was elected justice of the peace in 1876. A Republican, he ran for other offices on several occasions, including county auditor in 1878, receiving just nineteen votes out of nearly six hundred.[7] In later years, he was elected to a two-year term as probate judge in Idaho County, but was defeated for reelection.[8]

Vincent held a dozen jobs and appointed positions in and around Lewiston, among them town marshal, road commissioner, city assessor, restaurant owner, even town auctioneer—he listed auctioneer as his primary occupation in the 1880 Census. But except for justice of the peace, a position Vincent held for forty years in two Idaho counties, he seems not to have held any of his jobs for long. Whether this stemmed from a restless nature, or from an ambition overmatched by responsibilities—or undermatched by an overbearing personality—I can't say.

Vincent's dabbling in politics was reflected in his signature on a petition addressed to President Grover Cleveland on September 4, 1885, urging the appointment of Edward A. Stevenson as territorial governor—Stevenson received the appointment.

Vincent's singular achievement from a personal standpoint may have been to woo and wed Elizabeth Leland, the daughter of Alonzo M. Leland, publisher of the *Lewiston Teller* and a prominent businessman who arrived from Portland early in the Idaho gold rush to become one of Lewiston's biggest boosters. The Vincents were married in 1865 and had ten children.[9] They built an elegant home—likely financed with Alonzo Leland's money—on a 160-acre farm in a region called Tammany Hollow about eight miles south of Lewiston.[10]

Vincent had his quirks. He went out of his way to seek attention, perhaps as a result of living in the shadow of a prominent father-in-law. No publicity seemed beneath him. An example was this oddity in the *Lewiston Teller* on May 11, 1882: "J. K. Vincent of Tammany Hollow brought to town on Tuesday a young chicken with four perfectly formed legs. It can be seen at the post office where Joe has it in alcohol." A house-warming party for his new residence made the social columns of two newspapers. The *Teller* of June 8, 1886, noted that "J. K. Vincent has just completed a fine residence on his farm in Tammany Hollow. It will be dedicated tomorrow evening with a grand ball." The *Lewiston Tribune* told its readers that Vincent's party was "attended by merrymakers from all over the county," who waltzed and square-danced to music provided by a fiddler and organist.

Vincent's penchant for publicity might also have been an attempt to recover from an apparent failure of nerve early in his political career. When he arrived in Lewiston in 1865, the town was embroiled in great turmoil, resulting in ultimate humiliation. Fast-growing Boise in southern Idaho aggressively sought to wrest away Lewiston's status as territorial capital. As the conflict grew progressively heated, the town council appointed Vincent as a special deputy U.S. marshal to protect the territorial seal and other records against any attempt by Boise's backers to steal them. But Vincent failed in his assignment when Boise partisans, backed by soldiers from Fort Lapwai, raided the territorial offices. One account said Vincent was away from the city on business.[11] Another said he tried to repel the invaders, even chasing the men who took the seal, but was repulsed by soldiers.[12] Vincent offered his own explanation of why he didn't serve the court's order.

> *Not served on account of defendants being escorted by an armed body of soldiers commanded by Lt. S. R. Hammer, who resisted the service.*
> *J. K. Vincent*
> *Special Deputy U.S. Marshal*[13]

Vincent may have suffered from a healthy dose of cold feet. The raid on the territorial offices occurred while he was also serving as the appointed county sheriff, and his failure to save the territorial seal may explain why he didn't seek election when his term expired.

THE ROAD FROM Lewiston to Tammany Hollow led part way along a bluff overlooking the Snake River. Vincent, who traveled this road often, may have stopped on occasion to revel in the shifting seasonal colors of the wheat fields on both sides of the river, green in the spring and early summer, and sparkling gold before the late summer harvest. He might even have watched one fall day in 1886 as distant figures, wearing bulky tunics and wide-brimmed straw hats, pulled their boats south toward the mouth of Hells Canyon.

CHAPTER SEVEN

A Personal Journey

I NEEDED TO see where the Chinese died.

I had been in the canyon before, the first time on a five-day, four-night whitewater trip by dory down the Snake from the base of Hells Canyon Dam to Heller Bar, near the canyon's northernmost entrance, a distance of about eighty miles. The group I was with camped at night on the occasional postage stamp-size beaches along the base of the cliffs. It was a spectacular trip, providing an intimate view of the canyon's wonders.

On another occasion, a friend flew me the length of the canyon in his small Cessna aircraft, a hair-raising flight during which I clung to a loose side window—the latch was broken—to avoid being smacked in the face. I would also travel into the canyon later by jetboat with my wife, Candise.

But I had never hiked into the canyon. I lured a friend from Washington, D. C., Mike Shanahan, to make the trek with me.

While it would have taken the Evans gang much of the day to ride on horseback from the tiny community of Imnaha to Deep Creek in 1887, we could drive most of the way in a four-wheel-drive vehicle, reducing the time to a couple of hours. The road north along the Imnaha River is one lane, unpaved, deeply rutted in places, rocky in others. It is a spectacular drive, if occasionally hair-raising. We had a Jeep; I drove.

North of Imnaha, the road bridges the river and enters the Hells Canyon National Recreation Area. Once across the bridge, we followed the road up the Imnaha gorge's western wall, winding high above the river for the next ten miles. On the brief occasions when I dared take my eyes off the road, I could see the Imnaha River a thousand or so feet below, a ribbon of silver-blue winding between narrow strips of green. At one point, the north-flowing river seemed to turn on its side as it cascaded around a bend and plunged through a narrow opening where an ancient lava flow had nearly pinched the river in two.

We made the trip in early August, not the best time because of the summer heat, although a good time to see the slopes and canyon walls aglow with golden bunchgrass. On both sides of the Imnaha, the cliffs are layered with the flows of ancient volcanic eruptions. Far ahead of us, where the

Imnaha joined the Snake, loomed the mountain peaks of Idaho's Salmon River country. To our east, out of our view, were the saw-blade peaks of Idaho's Seven Devils Mountains, which form part of the eastern wall of Hells Canyon.

Returning to the canyon floor, the road crossed Thorne Creek ranch, then turned east across a narrow bridge and, leaving the river, switch-backed up a steep hillside to Lone Pine Saddle and over the lower slopes of Cactus Mountain, named for the prickly pear cactus which grow in abundance in the arid climate. From Cactus Mountain, the road dropped steeply into Hells Canyon. Rounding a curve, we got our first glimpse of the Snake, still several hundred feet below. We beheld a wide, strikingly bright blue river appearing almost phosphorescent against the canyon's dun and rust-colored basalt cliffs. The river emerged from around a bend to our south, remained in view for a mile or two, then disappeared again among the twisting canyon walls to the north.

The road from Imnaha provides the only vehicle access to the floor of Hells Canyon on the Oregon side for seventy miles. It ends at Dug Bar, identified by a Forest Service sign as the approximate river crossing of Chief Joseph and the Wallowa band of Nez Perce in 1877. With all that had happened at Dug Bar, it seemed incongruous, even irrational, that it carried the name, albeit abbreviated, of the rancher-outlaw, Thomas Douglas.

Be that as it may, Dug Bar is a wide beach of gritty grey sand formed in the backwash of the ancient floods that carved the canyon. It is maintained by the Forest Service as a campsite and boat landing. A mail box at river's edge receives twice-weekly mail service, delivered by jetboat from Lewiston, for a nearby ranch. Across the river, rising from the Idaho bank, is a unique volcanic feature: a thirty-foot high wall of vertical rust-colored basalt columns resembling giant fence posts, formed during cooling of lava following an eruption. Behind the columns, the cliff walls, largely devoid of vegetation, slope sharply upward.

ALTHOUGH HELLS CANYON takes a back seat to the Grand Canyon in term of its grandeur, it outranks its Arizona counterpart as the deepest canyon in North America. And for those who have traveled the canyon, its grandeur is stunning enough. Known as the Snake River Canyon until the mid-twentieth century, it was carved over millions of years by the combined effect of the river eroding layers of basalt, left from massive volcanic flows, and by later flooding from enormous inland lakes. Major shaping of the canyon occurred as recently as fifteen thousand years ago when Lake Bonneville broke though a natural barrier at Red Rock Pass near the present American Falls in southeastern Idaho, sending floodwaters crashing through the canyon on their rush to the Pacific.

The outpouring from Lake Bonneville, a remnant of which is Utah's Great Salt Lake, scoured a canyon ten miles across, with an average depth of 5,500 feet. At its deepest point at He Devil Peak in Idaho's Seven Devils Mountains, the canyon is 7,913 feet deep, measured from rim to river—by comparison, Grand Canyon's deepest point is 6,100 feet. The cliffs of Hells Canyon extend at least a mile high for forty miles. Layers of rust-colored and brown basalt from volcanic eruptions line the canyon walls, giving them the appearance of a layered cake left too long in the oven. Dark-colored rocks along the lower walls were once ocean floor-sediments and basalt from the volcanoes of the Pacific Island chain that joined the North American continent some one hundred and twenty million years ago, forming what is now Oregon.[1]

There are multiple cliffs, some along the river, others rising behind them in stair-step fashion. On the Oregon side, above the river cliffs, stretches a fertile half-mile-wide bench that slopes upward to a second tier of cliffs. Wallowa country ranchers—George Craig among them—trailed their herds from spring and summer pastures into the canyon in the fall, turning them loose on the bench where the upper cliffs protected them from icy winter winds. Within the confines of the canyon, however, the herds fell prey to the rustlers who operated with virtual impunity—nearly impossible to track down in the rugged canyon.

While large areas of the canyon look the same today as they did in the 1880s, the canyon is significantly changed in its use. Much of it was incorporated into the Hells Canyon National Recreation Area, established by Congress in 1975 to preserve the area's natural beauty. Administered by the U.S. Forest Service, the recreation area encompasses six hundred and fifty thousand acres, most of it in Oregon, with some overlap into Idaho. While dams upstream and downstream have submerged large sections of the canyon, the stretch of river along which the Chinese labored remains

Mike and the author drove a one-lane road north through this gorge to reach Dug Bar on the Snake River where they spent the night before hiking to Deep Creek and Chinese Massacre Cove. The Imnaha River is visible in the background (Photo by the author)

largely free flowing, protected from dam building by the recreation area designation.

The Snake is a major river, the thirteenth-longest in North America, extending for a thousand miles from its headwaters in Yellowstone National Park. It flows west from Wyoming, crosses southern Idaho to Oregon, turns north to form the Idaho-Oregon border, then the Idaho-Washington border until it reaches Lewiston, where it turns sharply west to merge with the Columbia. Along the way, it collects the flow of forty tributaries in six states. What is now referred to as Hells Canyon extends for about ninety miles. Thirty-two miles of the river are classified as wild under the Wild and Scenic Rivers act, and another thirty-six miles as scenic.

WE ERECTED OUR tent under the only decent-size tree on the Dug Bar beach. The tree was a gnarled hackberry, one of the few trees native to the canyon. With its leathery green leaves and knobby bark, it provided reliable shade. It looked old enough that I wondered whether Chief Joseph might have conferred beneath its branches with other tribal leaders before crossing the river in 1877.

We were glad for the tent. While we were grilling an evening meal, black thunder clouds suddenly appeared overhead. We had scarcely five minutes to rescue our food and retreat into the tent before rain descended in buckets, as lightning crashed around us. In twenty minutes the storm had passed and the sky was clear again. Although not normally superstitious, I found myself wondering whether one of the many ghosts inhabiting the canyon had sent us a warning. We spent a peaceful night.

Deep Creek was still three miles farther south. We faced hiking the rest of the way. While we could have reached Deep Creek along the river, the sharp lava rock, steep cliffs, and dense river willow and other brush make for treacherous footing. I was certain Blue Evans and his gang couldn't have gone that way on horseback. They would have taken the longer but easier route across the bench, the way we chose to go. Leaving before sunrise, we followed a rough Forest Service trail past the Nez Perce sign and a sagging wooden fence, and up a steep slope to the rolling grass-covered bench. My intention was to complete the round-trip by early afternoon, before the worst of the day's searing heat.

View of Dug Bar and the Snake River from the bench on the Oregon side of Hells Canyon, with Idaho cliffs in the distance. (Photo by the author)

Mike stops to remove burrs from his boots during a hike with the author down the Dug Creek draw to Deep Creek. Slowed by the rugged terrain, they faced hiking back during the intense afternoon heat. The author struggled with severe cramping. (Photo by the author)

Looking back from the high point of the trail, I was awestruck by the dawn breaking around us. Behind where we stood, light from the rising sun descended toward us down the upper cliffs, transforming the pre-dawn grey of dry vegetation into a widening blaze of gold, while below, the river and Dug Bar remained obscured in purplish shadow. Gradually, the sunlight reached the bench where we stood, nearly blinding us as it moved past, finally to ignite the canyon and the river, made once again phosphorescent. Ahead, as far as I could see, stretched the undulating bench, a broad expanse of green and gold, broken by an occasional tree-filled draw. Elk grazed in the distance, while a bald eagle surveyed the river from the brilliant blue sky, its outstretched wings gliding on updrafts from the warming canyon.

As we followed the trail south, the river disappeared from our view beneath one of the lower cliffs. After an hour of hiking in the open under an ever-warming sun, we reached a fork in the trail, marked by a sign post without any signs. One fork led down into a narrow brushed-filled draw toward the river, while the other continued south, winding over the bench into the distance. The trail down the draw looked uninviting. However, consulting a Forest Service map I picked up at the Wallowa Mountains Visitor Center in Enterprise, I concluded it was the path we wanted. Mike hoped I was right, because if it proved a dead-end, he informed me, he was turning back. The hot sun was making Mike surly. I was glad he remained with me, because I would soon need him.

Evans must have led his gang down this same draw, the first accessible path to the river after Dug Bar. Accessible, yes; conveniently so, no. The trail was clogged with head-high thistles and sumac, thick clusters of poison ivy, fallen trees, and rope-like vines. We carried long poles, cut earlier from lodgepole pines, to batter our way through the undergrowth, although at the cost of raising clouds of dust from pollen and decayed leaves that stuck to our skin and made breathing difficult. A muddy creek, largely hidden in the dense undergrowth, trickled underfoot, sucking at our boots. The map identified the creek as Dug Creek, also named for Douglas—his body supposedly was buried nearby.

We stopped often to rest, draining our canteens and picking burrs from socks and boot tops, all the while swatting at mosquitoes, which fed at will. We also kept a keen eye for rattlesnakes, which, we had been warned, lurked in the shade. During one break, Mike, a Vietnam combat veteran, experienced anxious flashbacks from that war, feeling as if he was once again patrolling blindly through the thick Vietnam jungle, fearful of imminent ambush.

Two-thirds of the way down, we lost the trail in the thick brush, and, after futile attempts to find it, we blazed our own trail by climbing along the rocky south wall of the draw—not a particularly smart thing to do, as the loose rock easily dislodged under our feet. It took nearly two hours to reach the river, where we collapsed on the riverbank. I was soaked with perspiration, and out of breath.

When we had regained some energy—I was in worse shape than Mike— we again picked up the trail, which followed the riverbank for the final quarter-mile to Deep Creek. The river trail proved easier going, although we were once again in the open with no shade. As we clambered around basalt boulders in the oven-like heat, our sweaty handprints evaporated in seconds.

Aside from rubbery legs, I felt no worse for wear when we reached Deep Creek, although considerably behind my schedule. Warned in advance about the intense mid-day heat in Hells Canyon, I had planned the hike so we would reach the camp by 8 a.m., giving us several hours to look around before we started back at 11 a.m., arriving back at Dug Bar no later than 1 p.m. However, because of the difficult hike down the draw, and frequent stops to rest, we were already more than an hour behind schedule. Mike wisely chose to cool off in the river, while I explored.

I am not sure what I expected to find. A bowl-shaped configuration of cliffs, less steep than I had imagined, formed a half-circle around the cove, which opened onto a wide gravel and sand bar, and the river beyond. At the back of the cove, Deep Creek emerged from the cliffs and meandered across the terrain to almost disappear into the gravel bar, before draining into the river. The stream was scarcely more than a yard wide and a foot deep, although it was no doubt much larger during the spring runoff. At the time of the massacre, the creek was also known as Dead Line Creek, a name given by Douglas, the rancher-outlaw, who years earlier had run a herd of cattle on the bench above the river cliffs. Douglas had warned the Nez Perce to keep their cattle south of the stream, ignoring their treaty rights to the land. The name he picked, Dead Line Creek, left no doubt about his intended consequence for anyone failing to heed his warning.[2] At the rear of

The Chinese gold miners at Deep Creek built this wall as part of a cabin-like structure extending from a shelf of rock once used by Native Americans. (Photo by the author)

the cove, a cluster of hackberry trees and mountain mahogany, another tree native to the canyon, provided some shade.

Given the horrible crime committed here, I had anticipated a gloomy, haunting place. But the sunlight filtering onto the stream through the trees made it appear almost pretty. It was as pleasant a place to camp as anyone could hope to find along this section of the Snake.

Not surprisingly, little remained to suggest a Chinese presence. I had been told the only visible sign of habitation was fragments of two rock walls, set against a cliff near the rear of the cove, which the Chinese used for a dwelling or for storage, according to a 1960 U.S. Forest Service inventory of the site.[3] At the time, I was unable to find the walls—a major disappointment—probably because I was nervous about the heat and searched less thoroughly than I would have otherwise. My disappointment was later partly eased when the reader of an article I wrote about the trip kindly sent me photographs from his own visit years earlier.[4]

On a later occasion, I would find the structure: two crumbling rock walls extending out from a slanted shelf of rock, creating an enclosure roughly ten feet by ten feet. The Forest Service determined the rock shelf once served as a shelter for Native Americans and was used by the Chinese.[5] The agency's inventory said the Chinese miners, after building the rock walls, may have covered the enclosure with a log and sod roof, long since gone. The remains of the rock walls are four feet tall at the highest point, and quite possibly were never much higher.

There are several unusual pictographs on the rock shelf that defy definition. The Forest Service experts thought they were of Native American origin. But later visitors must have altered the pictographs, possibly in a lame attempt to make them appear to be Chinese writing.

The Forest Service found evidence of diversion ditches along Deep Creek "where water was run for placer mining."[6] The ditches were not in evidence forty years later, or at least, I did not find them.

MUCH MORE REMAINED of the Chinese camp in the early twentieth century when a young boy, James Brewrink, visited Deep Creek, according to a copy of a scrapbook entry found at a riverside lodge. It was sent to me by Priscilla Wegars, the volunteer curator of the Asian American Comparative Collection at the University of Idaho. Brewrink said he was six years old when he visited the Deep Creek site about 1910 with his father and mother and a mining crew. Neither Wegars nor I can attest to the accuracy of the account, but Brewrink's description of the sleeping structure roughly corresponds to the rock shelter.

> *It was my first introduction to human remains and is clearly remembered. The camp area was clearly evident with broken iron pots and tools scattered at a cooking area. The location of a living area was evident. The sleeping shelter was the most interesting. A recess dug into the bank had clear remains of double decks on both sides of the recess providing eight bunk spaces. Shelf parts of the bunks were mostly fallen probably by reason of failure of leather like bindings which had rotted away or been attacked by rodents. The bands holding end post frames may have been bark or vines and were in condition to show the original intent of the structure.*
>
> *Dad and his crew collected five skulls and other bones and buried them as best they could with the tools available. I was at the site again in my high school days and felt confident of the recollection I have as a six year old.*[7]

THE GRAVEL BAR where the Chinese mined may have been significantly altered by the river over the years, and I can only describe it as it appeared on my visits. The bar is about fifty yards long, half the length of a football field, extending from a jumble of man-sized boulders upstream to a narrow sandy beach downstream. The beach ends at a fifteen-foot-high basalt outcropping that juts into the river like a retaining wall. The river in front of the cove is nearly a hundred feet wide, well over a man's head in depth, and too fast and treacherous for anyone to swim across without being swept a good distance downstream—Mike's plunge into the river worried me, even though he stayed close to shore. Across the river are the steep, treeless cliffs of the Idaho shore. The location seems a near-perfect place for an ambush, and proved so in 1887. The tranquility of Deep Creek may have lured the Chinese into a false sense of security.

THE GOLD THAT drew miners—Chinese and Caucasians alike—to the region consisted largely of small particles, or dust, known as flour or float gold, which washed into the gravel and riverbanks from upstream deposits over thousands of years. In the late 1800s, a pinch of gold between thumb and forefinger bought a miner a drink—nearly every store and saloon around the mining camps kept scales for weighing dust.

Miners employed several devices for mining along streams and rivers. Most common in smaller-scale mining were the pan, the rocker, and the sluice. Panning was the simplest technique—although the least efficient—and was used chiefly to assess a claim's promise. Rockers, or sluices, were the probable tools of choice for the miners at Deep Creek.

In its simplest form, the rocker, or cradle, was a wooden box, open at one end, attached to two rockers, with a screen over the top and slats or riffles tacked horizontally across the bottom. The rocker could be store-bought, or homemade. It might, for example, be fashioned from a barrel lid, cut in half. While the device could be operated by a single miner, it worked best with two men, one shoveling potentially gold-bearing gravel onto the screen and dousing it with buckets of water, while the second rocked the device to wash the smaller material, hopefully including gold, through the screen. The rocking motion kept the bulk of the slushy debris moving across the riffles and out the open end, while the heavier particles of gold caught in the riffles. Easy to operate and transport, rockers were widely used by miners throughout the world. However, this was tedious and back-breaking work. At almost any mining site, larger rocks, called cobbles, had to be removed by hand to give access to the gold-bearing material. Chinese miners customarily hand-stacked their rock tailings into what became known as "Chinese walls," still visible at many mining sites.

*Chinese mining on
The American River at
Mongolian Flat, California
in 1849. (California
Historical Society)*

A sluice, also known as the "long tom," operated on the same principle as a rocker, and often was used to extract gold from river banks that had once been part of old river channels. Built with boards, the sluice was configured at a downward angle, leading, for example, from the top of a river bank to river level. It could be of any length. As with the rocker, riffles were tacked across the bottom. A miner shoveled dirt and gravel into the top of the sluice and water flushed it downward, catching the gold in the riffles, while the debris drained out the lower end. Since a great deal of water was required, miners frequently dug a ditch from a nearby stream to divert water into the sluice. The diversion ditches noted in the Forest Service's 1960 inventory at Deep Creek were evidence that the Chinese employed sluices in their mining.

The same techniques are in use today. But whichever technique Chea Po's crew employed—and they may have used all three—they faced the additional handicap of working in near-freezing water, fed by snowmelt. Arthritis and other ailments were hazards for miners.

Trapping the gold in the pan, rocker, or sluice did not end the process. Sand and dirt inevitably mixed with the gold and had to be separated out. This could be accomplished with mercury—known at the time as quicksilver—which absorbed the gold, but not the unwanted material. Miners sometimes spread a quicksilver paste over the bottom of their rockers or pans. Because quicksilver was expensive, miners recycled it by cooking the mixture in a kettle-like device called a retort. As the quicksilver boiled into steam, the gold settled to the bottom of the retort. The steam, in turn, flowed through a hose into a bucket of water and reconstituted as quicksilver, to be used again. Gold so separated was known as retorted gold. There was a downside to quicksilver, however. Not only was it costly, it also could cause mercury poisoning.

HAVING MISSED THE rock shelter, I saw nothing on that first visit to reveal the makeup of Chea Po's camp. Typically, Chinese miners slept in rock huts or dugouts—shallow recesses dug into the cliffs and walled up in front with rocks. Some Chinese also used tents. There are various vague descriptions of the Deep Creek camp, among them an unattributed typewritten document given me by a former Wallowa County clerk, the late Marjorie Martin, who wrote that the Chinese built two rock cabins, one on either side of the creek—one for sleeping and the other for storage.

I spent three hours exploring the campsite, taking photographs and making sketches. I also picked up a two-pound rock for Candise, who collects rocks from interesting places.

By the time Mike and I started our return, it was nearly noon. Mike had had the presence of mind to cool off in the river. Foolishly, I did not. Except to quickly munch a sandwich in the shadow of a boulder, I had been exposed to the intense sunlight and baking heat most of the time. I wore a hat, of course, and I had the confidence of knowing we had plenty of water—I was carrying a portable water purifier I bought in Enterprise, an invaluable purchase, it would turn out.

It took a half-hour to reach the trail up the draw. I arrived at the foot of the draw drenched with sweat, and needing rest. Mike regarded me curiously, as the trail along the river hadn't been especially challenging. I had no explanation for why I felt so exhausted. Once we started uphill, the first cramp struck after only about fifty feet, attacking me in the back of the right thigh. When I stopped to massage it away, another cramp tightened my left thigh. I did my best to massage them both, and stumbled on. But soon the calves in both legs also cramped, then my stomach. Perspiring heavily and in pain, I could barely walk. Mike helped by carrying my backpack, clearing obstacles along the trail, and keeping me supplied with water, drained from the muddy creek through my portable purifier. Fortunately, I still carried my pole, which gave me something to lean on. Fortunately, too, entering the draw from the river, we managed to stay on the trail.

Only half way up the draw, I needed to stop every fifty feet or so to rest, sometimes less, collapsing where I stopped, as often as not falling into the poison ivy growing in abundance along the trail. Rising again on my cramped legs was as painful an experience as I have ever endured.

Mike grew increasingly worried, and, at one point when I lay prostrate along the trail, gasping for breath, he announced he was going for help. I would have appreciated help, but I also knew it would take Mike hours to find someone, and that any reasonable mode of rescue in that rough terrain would be nearly impossible. I also thought how much it would frighten Candise if she heard I needed rescue, and, of course, rescue would mean a hospital. She had been none too keen about my taking this hike anyway. I resolved to keep going. Step after painful step, fueled by great quantities of water, I finally reached the bench at the top of the draw about 2 p.m., two hours later than I planned.

We were again in the open, under the relentless sun, with another hour of hiking ahead of us—the temperature was in the nineties. But it was mostly downhill, and, despite frequent cramping, I made it back without too much more difficulty. The severe cramping, I determined later, was due to my loss of salt through perspiration. While I had packed a lunch, and made sure we would have plenty of water, I had, stupidly, not thought of salt.

As we drove back to Imnaha that evening, with Mike at the wheel, I told him I would understand if he didn't send me a Christmas card that year. I intended a joke, but Mike wasn't into humor at that point. I never did confess that the rock I picked up for Candise was in my backpack, which he carried. Mike will read about that here, I guess.

The soreness in my legs lasted a week. The worst case of poison ivy I have ever had lasted much longer.

CHAPTER EIGHT

The Mon-Tung Camp

EXCAVATIONS ELSEWHERE OFFER clues to what the Chinese camp might have looked like. There has not been a thorough excavation at Deep Creek—Bruce Womack, a retired Forest Service archeologist, told me the agency lacked the resources, partly because of the remote location. He said Deep Creek had been repeatedly scavenged by fortune-hunters and other miners, and anything of consequence was probably dug up years ago.[1]

An excavation at another mining camp called the Mon-Tung Camp suggested that Marjorie Martin's description of Deep Creek might have some validity. Mon-Tung was discovered largely undisturbed in 1989 on the banks of the Snake River near Twin Falls, Idaho, about two hundred and fifty miles upriver from Deep Creek. Archaeologists found remains of two rock cabins, one for living and one for storage.

Records of ownership, which survive, show Mon-Tung and a nearby claim were acquired from a Caucasian owner in 1871 by two Chinese miners, Ah Mon Mong and Tung Toek Tong, in lieu of wages owed them. From 1871 on, the camp was continuously occupied by Chinese until it was abandoned in 1890.[2]

The rock cabin was set against a cliff and partially dug into a dirt ledge, giving the occupants protection from the cold and wind. Rectangular in shape, the cabin was nine by eleven feet, not quite four feet high, with a single entrance. Nothing remained of the roof, which would have been made of tent canvas, or boards and driftwood. The cabin had burned, possibly from a fire set purposely after the last occupant died. A Bureau of Land Management excavation report suggested that fellow miners customarily set fire to a deceased Chinese miner's cabin and possessions, fearful that if anyone else moved in, the dead man's spirit might return and bring them bad luck.[3]

The artifacts and tools uncovered at the Mon-Tung site presumably were similar to those used at Deep Creek. Among them: an intact bamboo-pattern rice bowl, broken pieces of glassware, an 1863 coin from Hong Kong, cans for opium, an opium pipe bowl, a brown ceramic liquor bottle, two shovel blades, an axe head, a miner's candle holder, a mining pan, two perforated iron screens for rockers, two rock chisels, a rule from a scale, pieces of a cast-iron stove, a black powder keg lid stamped with the date of 1869, and pieces of a retort. There were also Chinese buttons, remnants of a grass sleeping mat, a metal frame from a carpetbag, a small winter green porcelain cup, a small flat piece resembling a poker chip, a rusted coffee pot, a copper tray, and a knife and spoon. Also found was a broken sarsaparilla bottle—sarsaparilla was used as a blood purifier and a cure for syphilis, but may also have found use as an antidote to mercury poisoning.[4] The discovery of opium cans and opium smoking paraphernalia was not a surprise, as opium use was common among the Chinese and not unlawful nationally in the U.S. until 1909 when Congress passed the Opium Exclusion Act.

An excavation at a nearby ash pit revealed some of the miners' diet: bones of chickens, grouse, sage hens, and quail. Chinese generally shunned beef, preferring pork. At some mining camps, they often kept live pigs for slaughter. Other foods preferred by Chinese included dried oysters, dried cuttlefish, sweet rice, dried bamboo, salted cabbage, Chinese sugar, dried fruits and vegetables, vermicelli, mushrooms, peanut oil for cooking, and tea.[5] Many of these foodstuffs were imported and stocked by Chinese merchants in the larger towns, Lewiston among them.

Chinese frequently pooled their resources to purchase a claim. In a not atypical transaction in July 1869, five Chinese miners bought a claim on Grimes Creek near Centerville in southern Idaho for two thousand, nine hundred dollars from its Caucasian owner. The purchase included "all tools, sluices, flumes, cabin and everything thereunto belonging."[6] In another transaction, Wang Yet, Ah Lang, and Mon Hay & Co. purchased claims on Grimes Creek for one thousand, eight hundred dollars from John Carroll and James Norton. The purchase included:

> *75 or 80 sluice boxes, hydraulic telegraph, about 400 yards of hose, 2 pipes and nozzles, 1 whip saw, 1 cross cut saw, 3 sluice forks, 5 shovels, 7 picks, 2 axes, 2 hammers, 2 augers, 1 plane, 1 spirit level, two mining hoes, 1 hand saw, 1 square, 3 gold pans, about 3,000 feet of lumber and four cabins and a blacksmith shop in said claims, and all the cooking utensils and all the improvements, tools and fixtures therewith belonging.[7]*

Chinese extracted gold from previously worked claims simply by reprocessing the tailings, or mining debris, left behind by white owners. They also had the advantage of being satisfied with less. While Caucasian miners insisted on a "white man's wage" of five to six dollars a day, it was said—probably in exaggeration—that a Chinese could survive on as little as twenty-five cents a day, with some left over to send to their home villages.[8]

Some Chinese did achieve financial success, whether at mining or in other pursuits. The name of Hung Wan Chung was included on an 1872 list of forty-eight "chief wealth holders" in Nez Perce County, those with property valued at more than one thousand dollars. Hung's property, not otherwise described, but most likely in Lewiston, was valued at two thousand, five hundred dollars.[9] In southern Oregon's Applegate Valley, a Chinese named Gin Lin ran an extensive hydraulic-mining operation on the Applegate River that made him a millionaire. An interpretive site, called the Gin Lin Trail, is maintained by the U.S. Forest Service at Gin Lin's former mining operation.[10]

Typically, however, as one barrier to the Chinese fell away, another rose to take its place. Idaho's Territorial Legislature, meeting in Lewiston in 1864, imposed a monthly mining tax on the Chinese of four dollars, raised to five dollars in 1866.[11] Mining taxes also were imposed in Oregon and California, although frequently resisted by the Chinese. Oregon sought to restrict Chinese mining even further. The state's 1857 Constitutional convention decreed Chinese couldn't own mining claims or land, or even work on claims, although, in practice, this was not enforced.[12]

CHAPTER NINE

Two Investigations

BRUCE EVANS WAS arrested by sheriff's deputies on May 30, 1887, five days after the massacre, but not for the massacre. According to Horner's history, Evans thought he was being jailed for killing the Chinese. Instead, he was arrested for rustling, specifically, for altering a brand, the same charge facing Titus Canfield. The massacre hadn't yet been discovered. Omar LaRue and Robert McMillan were served with subpoenas the next day to testify in the case against Evans.

Evans was placed under guard in a room on the second floor of the Fine Hotel on Main Street in the town of Joseph. Two weeks later, on or about June 15, he escaped, after faking a late-night need to relieve himself. The carefully planned escape was detailed in a deposition, given three months later, on August 24, by Thomas H. Humphreys, the deputy sheriff assigned to guard Evans and one of those who arrested him.

> *On or about 15th of June while I was acting as guard of Bruce Evans he requested to go to the privy. After he got there, he came to the door presented a six-shooter and told me to take a walk. This I was obliged to do. The door partly protecting him from me. He then left.*[1]

Evans' escape occurred almost simultaneously with the discovery of the first bodies near Lewiston.

TWO INVESTIGATIONS INTO the massacre were pursued from ninety miles apart, one in Lewiston and the other in Wallowa County, both half-hearted and with virtually no coordination or contact between them. Records and correspondence in the National Archives strongly suggest the two jurisdictions were unaware of what the other was doing.

Judge Joseph Vincent undertook his investigation from Lewiston at the behest of the Chinese, a few weeks after the first bodies floated out of the canyon in June of 1887. The investigation in Wallowa County apparently didn't get under way until that fall after George Craig, the rancher, discovered decomposed bodies in the canyon.

At first, I found it improbable that Oregon authorities had not already been informed by their counterparts in the Idaho Territory of the bodies found at Lewiston. However, as I delved further into the case, I came to believe that the murdered Chinese attracted so little concern in Lewiston that no one bothered to let authorities to the south know. Such an attitude might also explain why Vincent apparently didn't seek the help of any other law enforcement agency.

Moreover, there is nothing to indicate that Oregon officials took much of an interest, once they did learn of the murders. That isn't so surprising, since Oregon's governor, Sylvester Pennoyer, had been one of the leaders of an anti-Chinese crusade in Portland. The Harvard-educated Democrat was elected governor in 1887, a year after chairing an assembly of about a thousand agitators demanding the ouster of Portland's Chinese.

Knowing Pennoyer's feelings toward the Chinese, and the constituency he represented, he was unlikely to assist authorities in Wallowa County, even if asked. And no record has survived of his being asked.

FRUSTRATED BY THE inaction of local authorities, the Chinese turned to the federal government. I followed the lead of David Stratton, the retired Washington State University history professor, in researching State Department files in the National Archives. During two trips to the Archives' elegant glass-fronted building off a quiet residential street in College Park, Maryland, I found nearly two dozen letters and documents relating to the massacre, many of which Stratton had located before me. Now on microfilm, they include nineteenth-century correspondence from the Chinese legation in Washington, D.C., which had forwarded to the State Department the communications between Vincent and the San Francisco consulate. Among the correspondence was a letter to Vincent dated July 14, 1887, from Liang Ting-Tsan, the consul-general in San Francisco, and consul Frederick A. Bee, requesting more information after reading the initial Lewiston newspaper accounts of the murders.

From the outset, the consulate focused on ten dead, the number reported by the *Lewiston Teller*. It is not clear when, if ever, Chinese officials learned the full scope of the massacre. Vincent and other authorities in Lewiston may not have known either. Although the much larger number of victims, thirty-one or thirty-four, eventually became known in Wallowa County, there is no record of any direct communication between the Chinese government and authorities in Wallowa County concerning the number of dead, or any other aspect of the crime.

Even before writing Vincent, the Sam Yup Company had engaged Lee Loi to investigate the murders. Almost nothing is known about Loi's background—the consulate identified him simply as an interpreter living near Log Cabin Bar in the Washington Territory, where one of the bodies was found. His name appeared on several documents, showing that he was involved in the investigation, at least at the outset. Appearing before Vincent in the latter's judicial capacity on June 18, 1887, Loi swore out the following John Doe complaint against the unknown killers.

> *Lee Loi, first being duly sworn, complains and accuses Richard Doe, John Doe and others, names unknown, of the crime of murder by feloniously willfully and with malice aforethought cut with an axe, shot with a gun or pistol loaded with powder and ball, which they, the said Richard Roe and John Roe and others, names unknown, did hold in their hands, kill and murder ten Chinamen, belonging to what is known as the Sam Yup Co. Said murders having been committed on Snake River in the State of Oregon, Wallowa County, about 120 miles from Lewiston, Nez Perce County, Idaho Territory, on or about May 25th 1887 to the best of his knowledge and belief ...*
>
> > *Signed, Lee Loi*
> >
> > *Subscribed and sworn to before me this 18th day of June 1887*
> >
> > *J. K. Vincent*
> >
> > *Justice of the Peace of Nez Perce County, Idaho Territory.*[2]

Loi's name appeared again in an arrest warrant, issued by Vincent, also on June 18. And he was subsequently mentioned, by name only, in Vincent's letters informing the Chinese consulate of the progress of the investigation.

Most likely, Loi, or Lee, belonged to the merchant class, members of which received more lenient treatment under American law than laborers. Possibly he was born in the United States to parents who had immigrated earlier. While laborers didn't bring their wives—they couldn't afford to, and later were so prohibited by American law—merchants and other Chinese of higher rank could bring their families, and frequently did so.

Vincent replied to Liang on July 19, recounting what he had done so far, including, he said, making two trips into the canyon. Written in fractured English, this letter includes Vincent's last mention of Lee Loi.

> *I have been in Lee Loi's employ, have been up Snake River above where the murder was committed. Water so high, impossible to find out what was done. Since have made a trip to the Salmon River from which I returned yesterday. Today, I had a talk with a Chinaman who saw provisions on Bar [sic] after men were gone. I have been and am still in the employ of the Chinese Company [sic], ferreting out the matter. From what I have so far found, things seem to show that white men were the murderers, as some of the provisions "flour" I have traced directly to them. I have been following up, for 6 days, a white man who was at their camp and one who is the last one known to have been there. He has told some very curious stories about the matter and some circumstances look very suspicious. But there is in that vicinity some 20 or 30 bad men and I was watched very closely for 9 days. I expect to start again up Snake River on the east side and will get into their camp by some means and know what has been done with their property, if the agent here think best.[3]*

It was in this letter that Vincent revealed that the bodies showed evidence of torture. The letter is a rambling document that provided little meaningful information. For example, while Vincent said he heard "some very curious stories about the matter and some circumstances look very suspicious," he offered no hint as to what these were. His reference to flour apparently refers to flour taken by the gang from the Chinese camp. But how he identified the flour and traced it, he didn't say. Moreover, in his travel into the canyon, he apparently remained on the Idaho side of the Snake, never crossing into Oregon, where the murders occurred and the Evans gang operated. Indeed, there is nothing in the correspondence to indicate Vincent ever went to the massacre site.

Tucker, writing in his magazine article, credited Vincent for being far more aggressive in pursuing the case than official records indicate. He said Vincent, accompanied by a Chinese—probably Lee Loi—and another man named James McCormick, traveled into Hells Canyon to a point on the Idaho side just below Deep Creek. The article says that Vincent left the others and crossed into Oregon, disguising himself as a gold miner in an attempt to infiltrate the camp of a group of men "who appeared to have no legitimate business in the area."

> *Vincent set about panning gold and visiting the camp occasionally. He made friends with two young fellows whom he entertained with tales of the Mother Lode Country [sic] and a fabulously rich vein of gold which he knew about, but needed assistance to develop. Meanwhile, he asked innocent questions and picked up a lot of information.*[4]

In his dramatized account, Tucker also wrote that Vincent poisoned a dog belonging to Canfield in order to get close to the killers' camp at night: "He listened to conversations between the outlaws when an uncontrolled cough would have mean instant death or worse."[5]

However, there is good reason to believe Tucker was being more creative than factual. He wrongly attributed to Vincent the key role in the arrest of several gang members. According to his account, Vincent had gone to Wallowa County to persuade Frank Vaughan to confess and turn state's evidence against the others. However, Vincent's correspondence in the National Archives revealed he was in Lewiston at the time of the major break in the case, with no knowledge either of a confession or events that followed.[6]

CHAPTER TEN

"With Great Regret"

IT WASN'T UNTIL February of 1888, nine months after the slayings, that the Chinese legation in Washington, D.C., informed Secretary of State Thomas F. Bayard of the massacre. It may have been the first Bayard heard of it. Curiously, although Vincent had official status as a U.S. commissioner, there is no record of his reporting the crime to Washington any earlier.

One explanation for Vincent's reluctance to share information might be that he saw an opportunity to make money from the Chinese. The Sam Yup Company had paid him as much as one thousand dollars to investigate the crime, and in subsequent correspondence he would appeal for more.

As for the legation's delay in informing Washington, that may have been a consequence of Washington's tepid response to previous complaints of murder and abuse. The Chinese government had complained for years of other crimes against their citizens, seeking protection under provisions of two treaties, the Burlingame Treaty of 1868 and the so-called Angell treaty of 1880, but with scant results.

The Burlingame Treaty was negotiated for the Chinese by an American, Anson Burlingame, formerly the U.S. minister to China under Presidents Lincoln and Andrew Johnson. It marked a breakthrough in U.S.-Chinese relations. The Qing dynasty rulers, suspicious of the outside world, had long resisted American pressure for diplomatic relations. However, with trade between the two countries increasing, they gave in, at least in principle, and allowed the trusted Burlingame to negotiate on their behalf. The treaty cleared the way for an exchange of diplomats, and was hailed in the United States as portending a significant opening of Chinese markets to American exports. It also served to attract more Chinese laborers, still much in demand to work on the railroads.[1] Importantly for the Chinese, the treaty also included security guarantees for their emigrants, although denying them the right to become naturalized American citizens. Key provisions were Articles V and VI.

Article V. The United States of America and the Emperor of China cordially recognize the inherent and inalienable right of man to change his home and allegiance and also the mutual advantage of the free migration and emigration of their citizens and subjects respectively, from one country to the other, for the purpose of curiosity, of trade or as permanent residents. ...

Article VI. Citizens of the United States visiting or residing in China shall enjoy the same privileges, or exemptions in respect to travel or residence as may there be enjoyed by the citizens or subjects of the most favored nation. And, reciprocally, Chinese subjects visiting or residing in the United States shall enjoy the same privileges, immunities, and exemptions in respect to travel or residences as may there be enjoyed by the citizens or subjects of the most favored nation. But nothing herein contained shall be held to confer naturalization upon citizens of the United States in China, nor upon the subjects of China in the United States.[2]

Betty Lee Sung wrote in her 1971 book, *The Story of the Chinese in America*, that while the treaty ostensibly included benefits for both countries, the United States focused only on its own gains. "It was obvious that the nation's mind was on a single track, concentrating only on the benefits derived and not on the obligations assumed, for the United States was not only unprepared to assume the obligations, she was also unwilling. The ignominious treatment of the Chinese ... bear [*sic*] witness to that."[3]

Although the treaty provided for an exchange of diplomats, a decade would pass before China's rulers sent representatives to Washington, a delay partly attributed to the difficult transition of authority following the death of the Emperor Tongzhi (T'ung Chih) in 1875, and the succession of the boy emperor, the four-year-old Guangxu (Kuangsu).[4] It was not until 1878 that China opened its first legation at 2925 F Street in northwest Washington, D.C., soon to add consulates in San Francisco and New York City.

Unfortunately for both nations, American attitudes toward Chinese immigrants sharply deteriorated during the ten years between the treaty's signing and the dispatch of Chinese diplomats. As noted earlier, the 1873 panic, which caused several railroads to fail, brought lay-offs for thousands of workers of both races, throwing them into a desperate competition for the work that remained.

The time was ripe for demagogues, most notably Dennis Kearney, who founded the Workingman's Party of California, using it as a platform for anti-Chinese diatribes. Encouraged by San Francisco Mayor I. S. Kalloch, Kearney denounced the Chinese for "working hand-in-hand with monopolies, of accepting slave wages and of robbing the white man of his job." He typically ended his speeches with the cry, "The Chinese must go,"[5] a cry soon echoed among vote-hungry politicians in California and elsewhere in the West. Unemployed Caucasians staged nearly daily marches in San Francisco demanding the total exclusion of Chinese from American shores. A California Senate committee fueled the hostility by concluding in an exaggerated 1877 study that Chinese had taken one hundred and eighty million dollars in gold from California, while giving nothing in return.

The committee summed up its study in a so-called *Address to the People of the United States Upon the Evils of Chinese Immigration*:

During their entire settlement in California they have never adapted themselves to our habits, mode of dress or our educational system, have never learned the sanctity of an oath, never desired to become citizens, or to perform the duties of citizenship, never discovered the difference between right and wrong, never ceased the worship of their idols, or advanced a step beyond the traditions of their native hive [sic]. Impregnable to all the influences of our Anglo-Saxon life, they remain the same stolid Asiatics that have floated on the rivers and slaved in the fields of China for thirty centuries of time.[6]

During the next several years, anti-Chinese attitudes would harden.[7] Chinese already were being jailed and abused on trumped-up charges. Ordinances were frequently enacted to humiliate the Chinese, such as San Francisco's so-called 1873 "Queue" ordinance requiring that jailed Chinese would have their queues cut off. Many such ordinances would not stand, but the hostility behind these measures couldn't be more clear.[8] And violence was an-ever present threat. In 1871 in Los Angeles, nineteen Chinese were murdered, seventeen of them lynched.[9]

Under intense pressure from western politicians, President Rutherford P. Hayes prevailed on the Chinese to negotiate a new immigration treaty. Concluded on November 17, 1880, the treaty, known as the Angell treaty, authorized the United States to unilaterally restrict Chinese immigration.

But the Chinese government also received something it desperately wanted: a specific pledge of protection for Chinese immigrants who remained on American soil. Article III would be frequently cited by the Chinese government in years to come.

> *If Chinese laborers, or Chinese of any other class, now either permanently or temporarily residing in the territory of the United States, meet with ill-treatment at the hands of any other person, the government of the United States will exert all its power to devise measures for their protection, and to secure to them the same rights, privileges, immunities and exemptions as may be enjoyed by the citizens or subjects of the most favored nation and to which they are entitled by treaty.*[10]

The 47th Congress implemented the treaty by enacting the Chinese Exclusion Act of 1882, which barred further immigration by Chinese laborers, although permitting those already in the country to remain. The Exclusion Act did not apply to students, professionals or merchants. As first enacted by Congress, the act would have banned Chinese laborers, both unskilled and skilled, for twenty years. Supported by western and southern lawmakers, but generally opposed by those from the east, the bill passed the Senate by a vote of 29-15, and the House, 167-66, with 55 abstentions. But when the Chinese legation protested the length of the ban, President Chester Arthur vetoed the bill. Weeks later, Congress enacted a nearly identical bill, but with a ten-year ban, which Arthur signed on May 6, 1882. It was the first time the American government had restricted immigration on the basis of race and national origin. The preamble made no attempt at subtlety.

> *Whereas, in the opinion of the Government of the United States, the coming of Chinese laborers to this country endangers the good order of certain localities within the territory thereof; Therefore,*
>
> *Be it enacted by the Senate and House of Representatives of the United States of America in Congress assembled, that from and after the expiration of ninety days next after the passage of this act, and until the expiration of ten years next after the passage of this act, the coming of Chinese laborers to the United States be, and in the same is hereby, suspended, and during such suspension it shall not be lawful for any*

Chinese laborer to come, or, having so come after the expiration of said ninety days, to remain in the United States.

Section 12 stipulated "any Chinese person found unlawfully within the United States shall be caused to be removed therefrom to the country from whence he came."[11]

As harshly as the act came down against future immigration, its protections for the remaining Chinese seemed iron-clad. But seeming is not being.

CHAPTER ELEVEN

Rock Springs and More

THE HISTORIAN Shih-shan Henry Tsai wrote that, "For Chinese-Americans, the Exclusion Act of 1882 has become their ethnic Pearl Harbor."[1] Subsequent legislation would impose even more onerous restrictions.

The act succeeded in its goal of shutting down Chinese immigration. In 1882, the last year of unrestricted immigration, 39,579 Chinese crossed the Pacific to American shores, the most for any year. By 1883, with the ban fully in effect, the number fell to 8,031, and by 1884, just 4,009.[2] Some human smuggling continued, especially across the border from Canada.

But although the Exclusion Act effectively blocked new laborers, it failed to protect the estimated 132,300 Chinese who remained. If anything, violence and mistreatment became worse. Thousands of Chinese were driven from their homes and businesses across California, including from Redding, Eureka, and Truckee.[3] In San Francisco, white mobs set fire to Chinatown and murdered thirteen Chinese over a three-month period from September to November 1885.[4]

The highly organized anti-Chinese movement didn't just focus on California. Fueled by agitators, it spread like wildfire across the West.

In Tacoma, in the Washington Territory, a white mob encouraged by Mayor Jacob Weisbach, a German immigrant, evicted three hundred Chinese, during the winter of 1885.[5] Herded onto wagons, many were dumped in a forest far from town, where men, women, and children huddled in a cold rain while their homes and shops were sacked and burned.[6] Some would go to Portland.[7]

Violence also threatened the Chinese population in Seattle, resulting in several deaths. President Cleveland, acceding to a request from Washington Governor Watson Squire, dispatched soldiers from Fort Vancouver on November 7, 1885—the first use of federal troops to protect the Chinese.[8] On February 10, 1886, Cleveland ordered troops to Seattle a second time when Chinese were again threatened.[9] A white mob had forced about four hundred Chinese from their homes and marched them to the city docks to put them aboard a ship for California. Authorities intervened, but about half of the Chinese, tired of the harassment, still chose to leave.[10] Before troops arrived, a citizens' militia called the Home Guards fired on a Caucasian mob on February 8, killing or injuring five whites.[11]

Elsewhere in the Washington Territory, three hop-pickers were killed at Squak Valley and the homes of forty-nine miners were burned at the Coal Creek mine—both incidents occurred nearly Seattle in 1885. They were cited in a Chinese legation complaint to the State Department.[12]

Still in 1885, five Chinese were hanged by vigilantes after being accused of murdering a white merchant, David M. Fraser, in Pierce, Idaho.[13] In Anaconda in the Montana Territory, a mysterious explosion blew apart a Chinese restaurant, killing four Chinese.[14]

In Portland, nearly two hundred so-called delegates convened an anti-Chinese "Congress" on February 10, 1886, with the aim of setting a thirty-day deadline for the ouster of all Chinese from Portland and Oregon.[15] The city's Chinese population was then estimated at about four thousand.[16] Alarmed, Portland Mayor John Gates joined with state and county authorities to protect the Chinese by organizing a security force of more than one thousand, including seven hundred volunteers, seventy-five city militia, two hundred special sheriff's deputies, and seventy-five Army veterans.[17]

Gates' actions received strong backing from *The Oregonian* newspaper and its prominent editor, Harvey Scott. Citing agitators' success in ousting Chinese from communities in California and the Washington Territory, Scott predicted it wouldn't happen in Portland and issued a stern warning to the agitators.

> *The Chinese are here under stipulations of a treaty between their own country and the United States. That treaty is one of the supreme laws of the land. It is the duty of every citizen to serve and obey it, and the duty of the authorities, state and national, to enforce it. They therefore who are concerting measures for expulsion of the Chinese are proposing rebellion against the United States. From many localities, by unlawful proceedings, the Chinese have been forced to depart. This effort to expel them is now concentrated upon Portland. Here it will stop. Portland is a law-abiding city. It does not countenance rebellion. It will not suffer people who are here in pursuance of law and entitled to its protection to be driven away by force. ... If they persist, the actors will be arrested if possible, and if not will be shot to death.[18]*

Scott declared as bogus the argument that the Chinese were taking jobs from the whites agitating for their removal, because, he argued, those whites wouldn't do the low-wage work being done by Chinese.

Events occurred in rapid-fire succession.

February 22—Beginning about one o'clock in the morning, an armed mob of about sixty forced about forty Chinese from their homes in Oregon City. The Chinese were employed at the Oregon City Woolen Mills.[19]

February 22—That evening, a torch-bearing mob of seven hundred to eight hundred men paraded in an anti-Chinese demonstration through Portland, accompanied by a brass band.[20]

March 5—About fifty masked men descended in the early morning on a camp of Chinese woodcutters on Mt. Tabor and also attacked Chinese dwellings in Albina. Between one hundred and two hundred Chinese fled across the Willamette River to Chinatown.[21]

March 11—Five white men were arrested for the attacks in Mt. Tabor and Albina, but denied in court any involvement.[22]

March 12—About thirty armed whites, wearing masks or with faces blackened, attacked Chinese gardeners in Guilds Lake, burning several of their homes.[23]

March 16—Mayor Gates called a public meeting to address the violence. But the meeting was taken over by a large anti-Chinese crowd, which elected governor-to-be Pennoyer as its chairman and issued edicts declaring, among other things, that "the presence of the Chinese in our state is an unmixed and unmitigated evil."[24]

March 16—Gates' meeting retreated to another site where about twelve hundred citizens, including most of the city's leaders, vowed to "pledge our means and if necessary our lives" to maintain peace and order to protect the rights of the Chinese to live and work in the community.[25]

The aggressive stand by community leaders seemed to sap the anti-Chinese movement of its energy and the campaign soon dissolved, with the result that Portland would henceforth be seen as a safe haven for Chinese, so much so that Scott was able to write in another *Oregonian* editorial on March 25:

We have not permitted the mob to drive the Chinese away from Portland; though in their employments in the vicinity of Portland they have been a good deal molested. ...

The Chinese are in our Pacific states and territories in response to a demand for labor for development of the country. It is not rich people, nor great establishments that mainly employ them, but chiefly people of small means, themselves working people, who find use for their labor to do many things for which it is impossible to pay high wages. In a country like this, ... almost untouched, and where free land in unlimited quantities awaits him who is willing to take his subsistence from it, the Chinese laborer not only should not be in the way, but on the contrary may be made a help, to any honest intelligent and enterprising white man.[26]

According to Nelson Chia-Chi Ho, who wrote a history of Portland's Chinatown, "Portland, in fact the whole State of Oregon, became a refuge for the persecuted Chinese who were looking for less volatile environs."[27]

ANOTHER REPORTED OREGON atrocity that many dismiss as a myth allegedly occurred at the so-called Lily White mine, northeast of Baker City, where, the story goes, as many as one hundred Chinese gold miners were buried alive by a mine boss who dynamited the mine entrance rather than pay their wages. Another version was that thirteen Chinese miners were buried in a cave–in, and the mine boss declined to initiate rescue.

The U.S. Forest Service has maintained a sign, alluding to the event as a legend, near where the mine was supposed to have existed. When I wrote a newspaper story about Lily White in 1995, the Forest Service officials I interviewed voiced disbelief that it ever occurred.[28] So did historian Priscilla Wegars, who told me, "The bottom line is it would have been impossible for one hundred Chinese to disappear without a trace."[29]

Richard Harris, a Baker City businessman, who for years has been the leading proponent that the rumors of the atrocity might actually be true, told me in 1995: "There were lots of atrocities against the Chinese in this area, and a lot of plausible evidence it could have happened."[30] I had driven with Harris over unpaved mountain roads when we unsuccessfully sought to locate the site, which he believed was near a Forest Service training center in the Blue Mountains about thirty-five miles northeast of Baker City. He offered a ten thousand dollar reward to anyone who could prove or disprove the mine's existence. No one collected. Harris put the year of the incident as occurring between 1886 and 1889.

In a 2009 interview, the sixty-eight-year-old Harris, now retired, said he "absolutely" continued to believe that the incident occurred, although he thinks it now more likely that between thirteen and sixteen Chinese were buried alive, rather than the one hundred he estimated previously.[31] While Harris can cite little actual evidence of such a crime, he said he has located what he believes is the mine entrance. He said he found mining tailings and evidence of mining equipment. He said he also found the sole of a small shoe, which might have belonged to a Chinese.

IN VIRTUALLY EVERY instance where Chinese were victimized in the Pacific Northwest, they put up little or no resistance. One historian wrote they feared resistance would only make matters worse.

> *Throughout history, the Chinese immigrants in this country seldom,*
> *if ever, resisted the attacks, riots and violence of the whites … They*
> *seemed to understand it would be useless for them to stand and retaliate*
> *against the whites, not only because they were too weak to achieve*
> *success but also because the whites were their potential employers …*
> *Too, the fear of being deported also forced them to submit to whites.*[32]

BY FAR THE worst violence, prior to Deep Creek, occurred at Rock Springs in the Wyoming Territory, where white miners attacked and killed twenty-eight Chinese workers at a coal mine owned by the Union Pacific Railroad on September 2, 1885. At the time of the attack, relations had already been rubbed raw by the refusal of the Chinese to join the Caucasians—largely European immigrants—in a strike for higher wages. The spark that ignited the violence occurred when a mine supervisor, acting over the objections of white workers, gave the Chinese access to a particularly rich vein of coal. Fighting broke out, closing the mine. Hours later, a mob descended on Chinatown, a community of more than three hundred, and, in a twelve-hour orgy of violence, indiscriminately robbed and shot the Chinese, and set fire to their homes. Chinese investigators later summarized the violence—using the miners' own words—in a report to the New York consulate in 1885.

Some of the rioters went off toward the railroad of Coal Pit No. 6, others set fire to the Chinese houses. Between 4 o'clock p.m. and a little past 9 o'clock p.m., all the camp houses belonging to the coal company and the Chinese huts had been burned down completely, only one of the company's camp houses remaining. Several of the camp houses near Coal Pit No. 6 were also burned, and the three Chinese huts there were also burned. All the Chinese houses burned numbered seventy-nine.

Some of the Chinese were killed at the bank of Bitter Creek, some near the railroad bridge, and some in "Chinatown." After having been killed, the dead bodies of some were carried to the burning buildings and thrown into the flames. Some of the Chinese who had hid themselves in the houses were killed and their bodies burned; some, who on account of sickness could not run, were burned alive in their houses. One Chinese was killed in "Whitemen's Town" in a laundry house, and his house demolished. The whole number of Chinese killed was twenty-eight, and those wounded fifteen.[33]

Although survivors identified many of those responsible, none were prosecuted. This came as no surprise to Frederick Bee, the American attorney who served as consul in China's San Francisco consulate. Sent to Rock Springs to investigate, Bee called the investigation by territorial authorities a "burlesque."[34] Retaliatory disturbances broke out in China. However, with little expectation of punishment for the killers, the Chinese turned their attention to obtaining damages from the U.S. government.

CHAPTER TWELVE

"Deplorable in the Extreme"

THE HEAD OF China's legation in Washington, D.C., Cheng Tsao Ju, complained to Secretary of State Bayard in a letter dated February 25, 1886 of "a concerted and widespread movement to deprive the Chinese residents of protection and rights guaranteed by treaties."

Cheng enclosed a copy of a letter from the Chinese Merchants Exchange in San Francisco, dated February 1, 1886, in which the merchants complained that Caucasian mobs had driven Chinese from a half-dozen California towns, while local authorities failed to intervene. Cheng said Chinese everywhere in the West, but especially in California, faced "great dangers."

> *The situation is deplorable in the extreme. Chinese are driven from their homes, dwellings burned, property robbed, people murdered without effort by authorities to protect them. ... The Chinese people are absolutely terrorized and flocking to San Francisco where destitution, now exists among them.*[1]

In his letter, Cheng also sought indemnification for the property losses at Rock Springs—although not yet for the twenty-eight victims.

Bayard's response to Cheng would be chilling, both in its callousness and its barely concealed prejudice. A Democrat and former U.S. senator from Delaware, Bayard had been appointed secretary of state by President Cleveland in 1885 and was best known for resolving a serious dispute with Canada over North Atlantic fisheries. Earlier in his career, he was one of the so-called Peace Democrats who opposed President Lincoln's use of force to unite the country during the Civil War—although he was credited with helping convince Delaware not to secede.[2] More important for U.S. relations with the Chinese, Bayard was said to believe that unrestrained immigration from China threatened white control of the American West.[3]

In his reply to Cheng on February 18, Bayard placed much of the blame on the Chinese for the violence against them. After a pro forma condemnation of the violence, he wrote:

> *Causes growing out of the peculiar characteristics and habits of the Chinese immigrants have induced them to segregate themselves from*

the rest of the residents and citizens of the United States and to refuse
to mingle with the mass of population, as the members of the other
nationalities. As a consequence, race prejudice has been more excited
against them, notably among aliens of other nationalities who are more
directly brought into competition with the Chinese in those fields of
merely manual toil where our skilled native labor finds it unprofitable
to engage.[4]

Nevertheless, following the Rock Springs massacre, President Cleveland was under pressure to do something, and he supported Cheng's request for compensation in a message to Congress on March 2, 1886. He said that while the United States was not obligated to compensate the Chinese—in part because the government blamed the massacre on European immigrants— "the discreditable failure of the authorities of the Wyoming Territory to bring justice to the guilty parties" justified an indemnity.[5] He warned of the danger of more attacks, and suggested that the only solution might be to further curtail immigration of Chinese laborers.

Every effort has been made by this government to prevent these violent
outbreaks and to aid the representatives of China in their investigation
of these outrages; and it is but just to say that they are traceable to
the lawlessness of men not citizens of the United States engaged in
competition with Chinese laborers …

Race prejudice is the chief factor in originating these disturbances,
and it exists in a large part of our domain, jeopardizing our domestic
peace and the good relationship we strive to maintain with China.[6]

Congress approved an indemnity for the Chinese of 147,748.74 dollars on February 24, 1887, to cover the loss of property. It would approve a second and larger indemnity for the twenty-eight victims, and for a host of other crimes against the Chinese, the following year.

But the Chinese wanted more than indemnification. They also sought protection. Cheng, however, was unable to see the matter through. He fell ill and returned to China in April of 1886, replaced as minister by Chang Yen Hoon. It fell to the new minister to inform Bayard on February 16, 1888, of the massacre at Deep Creek: "It is with great regret that I have to bring to your attention another case of outrage inflicted upon my countrymen, which resulted in the murder of ten Chinese laborers in the most horrible manner."[7]

Chang's five-page letter enclosed the copies of Vincent's reports to the San Francisco consulate, along with Lee Loi's formal complaint and the John Doe warrant. Chang also provided the sketchy information about the victims, including the names of the ten dead from Punyu, the Cheas and Kongs. He said these ten were clansmen of four men who had survived, Chea Tse-ke, Chea Fook, Kong-Shu, and Kong Chun. At least one of these four, Kong-Shu, had also been mining in the canyon.

Chang told Bayard the victims went to Log Cabin Bar "in a boat loaded with provisions, accompanied by another boat manned by Lee She and others, for the purpose of seeking for gold." He erred in locating the massacre at Log Cabin Bar, which was in the Washington Territory, far from Deep Creek. The mistake no doubt resulted from the fact that one of the bodies had been found at Log Cabin Bar, as well as the difficulties posed by translating between two languages.

Chang said Chea Po's party had been mining on the Snake River since October of 1886 before "they were suddenly murdered by some unknown persons" the following May or June. He wrote that Lee She's crew, mining further upriver, had discovered the bodies.

> [W]hen Lee She and his party came out of the bar in their boat they found three bodies of Chea Po's party floating down the river and some provisions and bedding lying profusely at the entrance of the bar, and upon a search being made further, found Chea Po's boat stranded on some rocks in the bar, with holes in the bottom, bearing indications of having been chopped with an axe and its tie-rope cut and drifting in the water; that Mr. J. Vincent, commissioner of Nez Perces County, Idaho [sic] visited the scene of the murder and on examining the three bodies found a number of wounds inflicted by an axe and bullets; that the bodies of the others that had been murdered have not yet been found.[8]

Chang also wrote of another, possibly related, incident, a month earlier.

> [A] person named Jackson told a Chinese named Hung Ah Yee that he had witnessed some cowboys, eight in number, forcibly driving Kong Shu and his party out of the bar in their boat and throwing their provisions and bedding overboard; that Kong Shu and his party fled from them being afraid to offer any resistance; and that since he had

learned of the murder of Chea Po and nine others, he came to the
conclusion that the cowboys had committed the crime.[9]

Chang's information may have come from Lee Loi, although he didn't
say so. Significantly, Chang wrote that while Vincent had aided in the
investigation earlier, he had more recently failed to respond to requests
from the new San Francisco consul-general, Owyang Ming, for additional
information. Chang said the consul-general had offered a reward for the
killers.

He (the consul-general) is therefore fully convinced that the murders
must be white men (Americans), and further says that the commissioner
promised to write again to him if he should thereafter have secured
more definite information regarding the stolen property, but several
months have elapsed and he has not heard from him again, although
he (the consul-general) has repeatedly written to him. He (the consul-
general) has offered a reward for the apprehension of the murders, and
has ordered Chea Tsze Ke and Lee Loi to make inquiries, but they have
not yet discovered the names of the murderers.[10]

If Chang expected Bayard to offer any more sympathy than before, he was
disappointed. Bayard replied on February 23, 1888, that the information in
Chang's letter was "confusing and even contradictory" and could "afford
very little basis for the successful operation of the law."[11] He promised only
to relay the information to the governors of Idaho and Oregon.

Once again the buck was passed. The Chinese had no reason to believe
governments at either the national, state, or territorial levels intended to do
anything at all.

PART TWO

The "Innocent"

CHAPTER THIRTEEN

Vaughan Confesses

FRANK VAUGHAN MAY, or may not, have been one of the killers. But there is no longer any doubt that he witnessed the events at Deep Creek. At some point, probably early in 1888, he confessed to what he knew. He agreed to turn state's evidence and appeared before a Circuit Court grand jury.

Based on Vaughan's testimony, the grand jury on March 23, 1888, returned indictments for murder against Bruce Evans and five other gang members—J. T. Canfield, Hezekiah "Carl" Hughes, Omar LaRue, Hiram Maynard, and Robert McMillan.[1] In exchange for turning state's evidence, Vaughan was not formally charged, although he was arrested and released on bond.

I don't know what, precisely, Vaughan confessed to, or the circumstances that prompted him to speak out. Did he step forward on his own after struggling with his conscience? Or did he confess only after being confronted?

Findley wrote that one of the schoolboys—probably referring to Vaughan—confessed while in jail. And this is possible. But his sequence of events doesn't correspond to the public record. He reported that the confession occurred about six months following the massacre, after members of the rustling gang were taken into custody when the rancher, Fred Nodine, discovered his horses were being stolen.

> Among those who had been arrested for stealing Nodine's horses were
> four of the gang who were implicated in the murder of the Chinese
> miners. One by one the prisoners had been released on bail, and of the
> Chinese murderers [sic] only two were still in jail. One of them was
> the leader of the murder gang and also of the cattle and horse rustlers
> gang and the other was one of the school boys whose conscience began
> troubling him so badly that he dropped a hint to the sheriff about the
> Chinese murders.[2]

However, records show Nodine had discovered the theft of his horses prior to the massacre. The two men accused of stealing his horses, Canfield and Evans, were already in the process of being charged—Canfield was free on bail at the time of the massacre, and Evans would be arrested within a week, only to escape two weeks later.

The record of the Vaughan confession, if one existed, has long since disappeared from Wallowa County files. Also missing is any record of the county's investigation into the murders. But the *New York Times* carried what is apparently a summary of Vaughan's confession on its front page on April 29, 1888, under the headline, "Murdered for Their Gold Dust." Written under a Walla Walla, Washington Territory, dateline, the *Times* said the seven members of the gang, including Vaughan,

> *entered into an agreement nearly a year ago to murder these Chinese miners for the gold dust, which it was thought they possessed, and the men agreed that if any of the party divulged the plot, the rest should kill him. Hughes did not like the idea of committing the deed and would have no hand in the matter, but at this time he was stopping with the parties who committed the deed. A short time after that all the men but Hughes went down to the Chinese camp and opened fire on the Chinamen, killing them all, ten in number, and then put the bodies of all except two into the boat, which the Chinamen had and scuttled it. They then secured all the money and gold dust they could find, amounting to between $4,000 and $5,000, which was given to Canfield to sell for coin and after he got possession of it, he left the country and the rest of the party got nothing.[3]*

That we know additional detail of Vaughan's role in the massacre is due to the diligence of the late Charlotte McIver, the elected Wallowa County clerk, who, more than a century after the massacre, discovered a packet of missing documents in an unused courthouse safe. I read about her discovery in the weekly *Wallowa County Chieftain*, whose reporter, Bill Rautenstrauch, suggested the documents may have been hidden decades earlier as part of a cover-up.[4] I wanted to see for myself.

THE DRIVE FROM my home in the Portland suburb of West Linn to Wallowa County is long, three hundred and twenty five miles and six hours. I have made the trip nearly two dozen times, both to pursue leads on the massacre and also just to visit a place I've come to love. The trip offers visual rewards unmatched in the lower forty-eight states. For the first one hundred and twenty-five miles, the route I take follows Interstate 84 east through the Columbia River Gorge, eighty-five miles of which are a designated National Scenic Area. Towering basalt cliffs line both the Washington and Oregon sides of the river. Graceful waterfalls, including the awe-inspiring six-hundred-foot-high Multnomah Falls, course down the cliffs on the Oregon shore. The western half of the gorge is bathed by moisture from the Pacific Ocean and the land along the river is thick with Douglas fir. But after the highway passes around the northern shoulder of Oregon's section of the Cascade Mountains, the terrain is transformed into high desert. A change in climate takes place near Hood River, where summer-time sail-boarders dart colorfully back and forth across the Columbia's whitecaps, propelled by the famously stiff gorge winds. The skyline to the south is dominated by Mount Hood, the queen of the Oregon Cascades, its upper slopes blanketed in snow even in mid-summer. After Hood River, wet gives way to dry, and fir to sagebrush.

After another eighty miles, the Columbia River turns north into Washington, while Interstate 84 continues east, emerging out of the gorge and heading in a straight line across the Oregon desert to Pendleton, the round-up town, after which the highway switchbacks steeply up the treeless western escarpment of the Blue Mountains. Near the top on a spring afternoon, looking down from a quarter-mile-high viewpoint, the whole of eastern Oregon is below me in miniature—puffs of dust kicked up by tiny tractors plowing brown fields; eighteen-wheelers crawling along the interstate like caterpillars, with Pendleton, now a toy town, barely visible on the horizon.

I soon am driving again through thick forest, much of it on the Umatilla Indian Reservation. After thirty miles of mountain driving, the highway drops into the Grande Ronde Valley to the logging and ranching town of La Grande, where I leave the four-lane interstate and turn north on Oregon 82, a two-lane highway. The southern slopes of the Wallowa Mountains are in front of me; the northern slopes of the Blues behind. The highway winds with the Grande Ronde River for the next twenty miles through farmers' fields and small towns with names such as Island City, Imbler, and Elgin—places where more buildings need paint than don't—heading toward the westernmost shoulder of the Wallowas. Just beyond Elgin, a lumber-mill town boasting an impressive two-story brick building with City Hall on its façade, built in a more prosperous time in 1912, now worn and looking little used despite a sign identifying it as an Opera House, the highway leaves the Grande Ronde and shoots uphill for another eight miles, before turning sharply east and dropping through a hole in the mountains called the Minam Gorge, taking me on a steep descent of nearly a thousand feet to the Wallowa River, leading, finally, into the Wallowa Valley.

IF NORMAN ROCKWELL were still alive, he would find in the Wallowa Valley endless inspiration for *Saturday Evening Post* magazine covers. The visitor enters a mosaic of farms, grazing cattle, aging barns, and modest homes, all in the shadow of the awesome beauty of the snow-capped Wallowa Mountains. Here, people honk and wave at their neighbors. Clothing choices tend toward jeans and work boots. Neckties are a rarity. So were people of color, until a recent influx of Latino farm workers.

As valleys go, it's of modest size, about forty miles long and five miles wide. There are four towns: Wallowa, Lostine, Enterprise, and Joseph, spaced roughly ten miles apart, from northwest to southeast, like beads on a string. None is large enough to require a traffic light, although all but Lostine boasts its own high school. Enterprise, the county seat, is first among equals, with a population of 1,895 in the 2000 Census, claiming the valley's only Safeway and a Best Western Motel.

Highway 82 leads across the valley to the town of Joseph, known for its bronze foundries and western-themed sculptures, some of them tastefully displayed on street corners. The town abuts four mile-long Wallowa Lake, a unique and captivating body of water that is one of the valley's true marvels. On a bright day, the lake resembles a huge purple amethyst, set between two mountains, and secured by a horseshoe-shaped moraine. More than most, Wallowa Lake is sensitive to any change in light so that its surface may turn in an instant from a bright blue to black. The moraine is an enormous bank of dirt and rock, gouged out of the mountains by ice-age glaciers. Rising almost a thousand feet, the moraine appears so uniform that first-time viewers can be forgiven for assuming it's a manufactured dike. In spring and early summer, portions of the moraine are blanketed by the brilliant yellow blossoms of the balsamroot, once a staple of the Nez Perce diet.

*The Wallowa Valley is nestled at the foot of the Wallowa Mountains in
northeastern Oregon. The forty-mile-long valley remained off-limits to white
settlement until a fraudulent treaty took it away from the Nez Perce. (Photo by
Elane Dickenson)*

The Wallowa River flows out of the lake to wind lazily back across the
valley, roughly paralleling Highway 82. The name Wallowa, appended
liberally to major and not-so-major features throughout the valley, is derived
from a Nez Perce word describing a structure of stakes set in a triangle, part
of a fish trap used by the Wallowa band of Nez Perce.[5]

Thirty miles east of the Wallowa Valley, through a narrow canyon, is the
smaller Imnaha River Valley, and its single small community, Imnaha—the
name is derived from a Nez Perce word that roughly translates to "Chief
Imna's land."[6] The picturesque hamlet, reached by a bridge across the
Imnaha River, consists of a dozen or so residences, a tiny post office, a
school, a combination tavern and store, and little else. The tavern/store for
years drew tourists to its annual rattlesnake roast, until crowds grew too
large for the town to handle.

NOTHING IN THE down-home lifestyle of Wallowa County's inhabitants hints at the great blemish on the region's history, the expulsion of the largely peaceful Nez Perce in 1877. I knew the story from the excellent history written by the late Alvin M. Josephy Jr., *The Nez Perce Indians and the Opening of the Northwest*. It's not a reach to suggest that the suspicion once directed toward the Nez Perce in the late 1800s extended to anyone who looked appreciably different, such as someone with a different skin tone, wearing their hair in a long braid, speaking an unintelligible language, and removing gold some whites might believe was rightfully theirs. All of this is conjecture, of course. But what I came to be certain of is that people in the county, important people, turned a blind eye to the massacre of the Chinese miners.

I relate what follows to suggest that trauma from the conflict with the Nez Perce was still fresh in the minds of the original settlers as they pondered the murder of unwanted intruders onto land previously seized from the Native Americans.

A TREATY SIGNED in 1855 had recognized a Nez Perce domain over a vast area of southeastern Washington, north central Idaho, and northeastern Oregon, a region that included both Lewiston on the north and the Wallowa Valley on the south. The Nez Perce were a collection of loosely affiliated bands with a combined population of possibly four thousand to six thousand.[7] One explanation for the name Nez Perce is that it was given by French-speaking trappers after they saw some tribal members wearing bits of decorative shells in their noses.[8] The tribe's name for themselves is Nimi'ipuu, meaning "the real people" or "we the people."[9]

At the time the government negotiated the 1855 treaty, settlers had little interest in the Wallowa Valley, despite its potential for farming and ranching. It was too remote for pioneers plying the Oregon Trail one hundred miles to the south, heading to the fertile Willamette Valley, west of the Cascades, and, nearer at hand, the Grande Ronde Valley.

However, outside interest in the Wallowa country was soon to grow—as interest already had in the gold-mining country on Nez Perce lands in what would become, in 1863, the Idaho Territory. The influx of thousands of miners into and around Lewiston brought pressures on the government to supplant the 1855 treaty.[10] And, in 1863, a new treaty was imposed—negotiated is too kind a word. Highly unfavorable to the Nez Perce, it reduced their lands to little more than one-tenth the size of the 1855 treaty lands—from 10,000 square miles to 1,290 square miles—on a new reservation at Lapwai, east of Lewiston. In return, the Nez Perce were to receive eight cents an acre for their surrendered land, a total of 265,000 dollars, not all of which would be paid. Josephy wrote of this "fraudulent act":

> *Taken from the Nez Perce were all of the Wallowa, Imnaha, and Grande Ronde country of Oregon, the valleys of the Snake and Salmon rivers, including such places as Asotin and Alpowa, the Camas Prairie, the upper waters of the Clearwater and its tributaries, and the trails to the Bitterroot Valley. By the treaty's terms, all the bands were required to move onto the reservation within one year after the document was ratified.*[11]

A number of Nez Perce chiefs succumbed to pressure, threats, or bribes—or all three—and agreed to move their bands onto the reservation. However, a few resisted, among them the elder Chief Joseph, leader of the Wallowa band of Nez Perce, for whom the Wallowa country had been a vital part of its homeland for thousands of years. Joseph, or Tuekakas to the Nez Perce, placed stone boundary markers outside the Minam Gorge to underscore his band's claim to the valley. Settlers knew the markers as "Old Joseph's Dead Line."[12] On his deathbed in 1871, the elder Joseph is said to have exhorted his son, the young Chief Joseph, or Hin-mah-too-yah-lat-kekht—Thunder Traveling to Higher Places—never to surrender the valley. With young Joseph as their chief, the Wallowa band, whose numbers were estimated at about three hundred, stayed put.[13]

However, pressures on the small band escalated. By the late 1860s, new arrivals along the Oregon Trail found fertile land with access to water increasingly scarce. When severe drought threatened crops and cattle on the farms and ranches in the Grande Ronde Valley, ranchers cast covetous eyes on the remote but well-watered valley over the Wallowa Mountains—known at the time as the Eagle Mountains—to the north.[14] The break in what had been a stand-off came in 1871, when two white ranchers from the Grande Ronde Valley, William McCormack and Neil Keith, ignored Old Joseph's markers and drove their herds through the Minam Gorge to graze in the Wallowa Valley. The Nez Perce didn't try to stop them, and when word got back that the ranchers met no resistance, dozens of settlers soon followed. They put up fences, ran their cattle, built homes. By July of 1873, some eighty-seven settlers had claimed land, and work had started on roads and irrigation ditches.[15]

The arrival of settlers forced the government's hand, as Washington had been confused over what should be done with the Wallowa country. The 1863 treaty wasn't ratified until 1867, and in 1873, President Ulysses Grant issued an executive order designating part of the valley as a Nez Perce reservation. Grant's order brought a storm of protest from the settlers, backed by strong political support from Oregon Governor Lafayette Grover and U.S. Senator James Slater, both Democrats.[16] Grant reversed himself two years later, and issued a new executive order that officially opened the valley to settlement in 1875.

Settlers acquired land in the Wallowa country in one of two ways, both authorized by the 1862 Homestead Act, enacted by Congress during the Civil War. Under the act, a head of family was entitled to one hundred and sixty acres, for which he or she could gain ownership by building a dwelling, cultivating the land, and living on the land for five years, a process commonly known as "proving up." A second method was to live on the land for six months, make minimal improvements, and pay the government one dollar and twenty-five cents an acre, a procedure called "pre-emption."[17]

THE NEZ PERCE had a reputation for being peaceful and generally friendly—one band in Idaho had provided valuable help to the Lewis and Clark expedition in 1805—and the Wallowa band sought to live alongside the settlers without conflict. Young Joseph withdrew the Nez Perce to corners of the valley not yet claimed by whites. Many settlers, too, sought to co-exist with the Wallowa band. However, conflict proved inevitable. In the spring, when the Nez Perce returned to the Wallowa Valley from winter camps in canyons to the north, some of the younger men insisted on going where they pleased, disregarding settlers' property lines. Fences were knocked down; horses were stolen or ran away; crops were trampled. On the Nez Perce side, tipi poles—customarily left behind during the Nez Perce' winter migration for use on their return—disappeared. Worse, a Nez Perce was shot and killed in a dispute over allegedly stolen horses. Ross Findley wrote that his father, Alexander Findley, fired the fatal shot in what was later ruled self-defense.[18]

Settlers cowered in their homes fearing an Indian attack that never came. Finally, in 1877, the Army sent two companies of soldiers from Fort Walla Walla, one hundred miles to the north, to enforce the 1863 treaty. They were under the command of General Oliver Otis Howard, a general who had lost his right arm in battle during the Civil War. Howard's instructions were to remove the Wallowa band to the reservation at Lapwai, even though Howard himself had once argued to Washington that the valley should remain in the hands of the Nez Perce. On May 14, 1877, Howard gave Joseph thirty days to move his band to the reservation.[19]

THE NEZ PERCE faced crossing the Snake River at Dug Bar, three miles upstream from where the Imnaha River enters the Snake. But it was late May, and the river raged from spring snowmelt. Chief Joseph sought a delay until the water subsided. But Howard was adamant. A deadline was a deadline.[20] One company of soldiers, about a hundred men, was camped near the mouth of the Grande Ronde, north of Dug Bar, armed with the feared Gatling Gun, a machine gun developed during the Civil War.[21]

With any thoughts of resistance futile, Joseph and his fellow chiefs bundled women, children, and the elderly into buffalo hide boats, which were led through the swift current by men on horseback. Miraculously, the entire band of several hundred safely reached the Idaho shore during the two-day crossing. Not so, the Nez Perce's livestock. Carcasses of cattle and horses washed up on downstream river banks for weeks and months, in the same way Chinese bodies would appear ten years later. An undetermined number of cattle and horses were left behind, falling into the hands of settlers, along with other Nez Perce possessions.[22]

While the crossing was peaceful, the aftermath was not. Once across, on June 2, Joseph was joined on the Idaho side by other so-called non-treaty bands, swelling his numbers to about six hundred, of whom more than two-thirds were women, children, and old men. Fighting would begin days later after renegade members of the band killed several white settlers in the Idaho Territory.[23] Rather than face punishment, Joseph and the other chiefs, some more militant than Joseph, decided to run for it, hoping to find refuge in Canada. Other Native Americans had fled to Canada before them, among them the Sioux chief, Sitting Bull. The Nez Perce fought off pursuing soldiers for four months and one thousand, seven hundred miles, until, bloodied and exhausted, they were cornered in a blizzard in Montana's Bear Paw Mountains, only forty miles short of the Canadian border. Chief Joseph surrendered on October 5, 1877. The soldier-poet C. E. S. Wood famously quoted Joseph as declaring in a surrender speech: "Hear me, my chiefs! I am tired. My heart is sick and sad. From where the sun now stands, I will fight no more forever."[24]

Both sides suffered hundreds of dead and wounded. Joseph's Nez Perce had been joined by other Native Americans, for a total of about seven hundred and fifty who fled toward Canada ahead of the Army. Of these, Josephy wrote at least one hundred and twenty were killed, including sixty-five men and fifty-five women and children. He put casualties among the Army and other pursuers at one hundred and eighty dead and one hundred and fifty wounded. Of the Nez Perce warriors, Josephy wrote: "Man for man, they had proven themselves better fighting men and marksmen than the soldiers or volunteers, many of whom were poor shots and had no stomach for combat."[25] Some did escape into Canada.[26]

The captured Nez Perce, Joseph among them, were exiled to the Indian Territory in present-day Oklahoma and later dispersed to several Pacific Northwest reservations. There was no further hindrance to white settlement in the Wallowa country.

KNOWING THIS HISTORY, it was with some considerable cynicism that on trips to the valley I would drive past signs lauding the valley's Nez Perce heritage. The names Wallowa and Joseph appear everywhere in the county. An annual rodeo and festival known as Chief Joseph Days is held, of course, in Joseph.

CHAPTER FOURTEEN

"Don't Ask . . . Don't Tell"

BUILT IN 1909, the Wallowa County Courthouse in Enterprise is a squat and, to me at least, architecturally uninteresting building, with walls of thick blocks of grey volcanic tuff. The tuff is a soft but durable rock known locally as Bowlby stone, cut from a nearby quarry. Other buildings around the courthouse square—housing a bookstore, an antique shop, a bar, restaurant, and law offices—are constructed of the same grey stone, giving downtown Enterprise something of the appearance of a military fort. The courthouse is two and one-half stories, topped by a white-washed wooden bell tower. Even without the bell tower, it is the tallest building in town.

The events of 9/11 raised no terrorist alarm here: there is no security check at any of the several courthouse entrances, although a security screen is positioned outside the second-floor courtroom. No one challenges, questions, or pays any attention as a stranger walks up the front steps and through the swinging front doors.

Inside, I discover that what the courthouse lacks in architectural elegance, it makes up in rustic charm. Floors, stairs, and wall trim are of red fir, worn but well maintained. Among the few concessions to modernity are copying machines, computers, and portable window air conditioners. There's no elevator, and no room for one. Disabled residents with courtroom business are carried by sheriff's deputies to the second floor.

My business was with Charlotte McIver, whose office shared the cramped first floor with the offices of the sheriff, treasurer, and county assessor. Unlike government officials in Washington, D.C., where I worked for fifteen years as a reporter with The Associated Press, McIver was immediately available and helpful. No appointment needed; no aide rushing forward to inquire of my business, or monitor our conversation.

Matronly and soft-spoken, McIver didn't hesitate to show me the long-forgotten trial records. She had found them while cleaning out an old safe, preparing to donate it to the county museum in Joseph. The documents were in brown envelopes, some discolored and brittle. McIver had no idea what they were at first. But leafing through the papers, she discovered many related to an 1888 murder trial, *State of Oregon versus Hyram* (sic)

The Wallowa County clerk who found the missing records of the massacre and trial in an unused county safe in 1995. She said her predecessor, Marjorie Martin, who admitted hiding the records, was trying to "to protect the interests of the county." (Photo by Elane Dickenson, Wallowa County Chieftain)

Maynard, Hezekiah Hughes indicted under the name of Carl Hughes and Robert McMillan jointly indicted with T. J. [sic] Canfield, Bruce Evans and C. O. Larue (sic).

"We didn't even know these records were missing," said McIver, who, like nearly everyone else in the county, knew little about the massacre and even less about the trial. The documents should have been in the large walk-in vault adjacent to McIver's office. By the time we talked in 1995, she had returned the documents to their rightful place, in an olive-colored metal box in the left-hand corner on the top shelf, the first box in the vault. "The county's first murder trial," she said.

Until McIver decided to dispose of the bulky safe, it sat unused for years in full view in a corner of the documents room adjacent to the clerk's office. Manufactured by the Diebold Safe and Block Company of Canton, Ohio, the safe had an uncertain history. The name of the long-gone Enterprise State Bank was printed in gold leaf on black paint above ponderous eight-inch-thick steel doors. The doors weren't easy to open, perhaps explaining why the safe had gone unused. When last I saw it, the safe was gathering dust in a museum storage room in Joseph.

While McIver wasn't comfortable in speculating that the missing records had been purposely hidden, then-County Judge Ben Boswell, the county's top elected official, had no such qualms. "Somebody didn't want those records found," Boswell told me an interview, the first of several. "Somebody intentionally caused people to forget."[1]

Boswell's knowledge of the county ran deep. He was a direct descendant of a pioneering family. His great-grandfather, also named Ben, settled in the valley in 1876 and operated a livery stable in Enterprise. Boswell's great-grandmother, Ellen Boswell, was among the first white women in the valley. His wife's great-grandfather, William Wilson, served as a county commissioner. So did his grandfather on his mother's side, George Dawson, whose picture was on the wall of Boswell's closet-sized office. Typical of many county residents, Boswell, then age forty-nine, had cobbled together a modest living from various jobs. Besides county judge, he had been a rancher, a high school science teacher, and part-time bus driver. At one time, while still a county judge, he commuted weekly to Eastern Oregon University in La Grande, a one hundred and twenty-mile round-trip, to teach physical education. His politics were Republican in the overwhelmingly Republican county.

Boswell said he had been as surprised as everyone else to learn of the forgotten documents and, despite his family background in the county, knew little about the murders. What he did know came from stories his father had told him when he was ten or so. "Dad said the killers laid in wait and shot the Chinese as they came out of their tents, one at a time"—yet another version.

Boswell recalled being among a group of Boy Scouts who once played a local version of the childhood game of "cowboys and Indians" at the massacre site. "We play-acted the massacre and divided up into cowboys and Chinamen. ... We had a hard time finding guys who wanted to be Chinamen."

Boswell told me there had long been the perception that many people who settled in Wallowa County "were on the run from somewhere else" and played fast and loose with the law, so few cared about their conduct at the time. "Around the turn of the (nineteenth) century, the morals kind of changed. That's probably when the cover-up occurred." I used his quotes in an article I wrote for *The Oregonian*.[2]

Boswell would later revise his remarks, although acknowledging he had been correctly quoted. "It wasn't so much a cover-up, as there just wasn't much interest in it," he told me. "It was just forgotten, not remembered ... kind of a non-event. I think the community didn't try to keep it secret [although] there may have been certain individuals who did." On another occasion, Boswell referred to what he called "The code of Wallowa County: 'You don't ask and you don't tell'."[3]

ON THAT FIRST VISIT, McIver left me alone to read the documents, which were not an easy read. Some were folded neatly in individual envelopes; others were loose and unorganized. The ink on some had faded to the point of being indecipherable. A further complication was they were handwritten in a looping stylized script, many with W's that look like H's—the style at the time.

Among the documents was the two-page indictment, dated March 23, 1888, in which a Circuit Court grand jury charged six men and teenagers with murdering ten Chinese. Named in the indictment were Bruce Evans, J. T. Canfield, Omar LaRue, Carl [Hezekiah] Hughes, Hiram Maynard, and Robert McMillan.

The indictment also listed names of ten victims, although these were names much different from the victims identified by the Chinese legation in its correspondence with the State Department. Whomever prepared the indictment acknowledged the names were made up. The indictment said the accused

acting together on the first day of May A.D. 1887 in the county and state aforesaid, purposely feloniously and of deliberate and premeditated malice killed Ah Jim, whose real name to the grand jury is unknown, and Ye Lee, whose true name to the grand jury is unknown, and Wy See, whose real name to the grand jury is unknown, and Hop Sing, whose true name to the grand jury is unknown, and Hee Lee, whose real name to the grand jury is unknown, and La Bate, whose real name to the grand jury is unknown, and Him Lim, whose real name to the grand jury is unknown, and He Gee whose real name to the grand jury is unknown, and Sing Him, whose real name to the grand jury is unknown, and Hop Gee whose real name to the grand jury is unknown, by shooting them ... with a rifle, contrary to the statutes in such cases, made and provided and against the peace and dignity of the State of

Oregon, dated at Joseph in the county aforesaid, the 23rd day of March AD 1888.[4]

Whether any attempt was made by Wallowa County authorities to learn the true identities of the victims isn't known, but it seems unlikely, given the lack of communication, and concern, among the several jurisdictions. The indictment mistook the date of the murders, mentioned in other documents as May 25.

CHAPTER FIFTEEN

A Story Changes

YOUNG FRANK VAUGHAN, once so trusted he was deputized to serve a subpoena on Bruce Evans, proved to be the key to sorting through the confusing twists and turns of the massacre story. Less than a month after his grand jury testimony brought indictments for murder against the six other gang members, he changed his testimony.

Of all the documents found in the safe, the most revealing was a deposition Vaughan gave on April 16, 1888, before County Judge Peter O'Sullivan. The deposition was taken at the request of the attorney defending the three gang members in custody, Hezekiah Hughes, Hiram Maynard, and Robert McMillan.

While the grand jury indictment had said the six gang members were "acting together," Vaughan stated in this deposition that he hadn't meant to leave that impression. He shifted all the blame to Evans, Canfield, and LaRue, the three who fled. He said neither he, nor Hughes, nor Maynard, nor McMillan, played any role in the killings. These three also gave depositions, declaring their innocence.

Vaughan's deposition is longer and more detailed than the others. The written text is not conversational in tone, so it is not verbatim and must have been prepared from notes. It begins with an unidentified defense attorney asking Vaughan about the involvement of Maynard, Hughes, and McMillan, after which Judge O'Sullivan takes over the questioning.

Question [Attorney]: State to the judge all you know about the guilt or innocence of Robert McMillan, H. Maynard, and H. K. Hughes concerning the killing of some Chinamen on Snake River, in this county and state, about a year ago.

Answer. Vaughan: Mr. Maynard and Mr. Hughes knew nothing of the circumstances before or after the killing to the best of my knowledge. Maynard and Hughes were about three miles from the place at the time. They were not present when any arrangements were made to do the killing.

The killing occurred as nearly as I can remember about the last of May. No arrangement to do the killing was made before we left the cabin. Bruce Evans, J. T. Canfield, Omar LaRue, Robert McMillan, and myself were the parties, and the only parties, that left the cabin. Maynard and Hughes remained at the cabin. The cabin was about three miles from the place of the killing.

All the persons named above, except Maynard and Hughes, were present at the time of the killing.

All the shooting done in killing those Chinamen was by other parties than Maynard, Hughes, McMillan, and myself. McMillan and myself were present, but had no means of preventing the affair.

Knowing that the parties who did the killing were desperate men, I hesitated about making the matter known before.

Q. [Judge O'Sullivan]: *You say that there were no arrangements made at the cabin. When were the arrangements made?*

A. *There was some talk of what they were going to do at Dead Line Creek, but no arrangements were made.*

Q. *What was this talk?*

A. *I don't recollect what it was. I didn't understand from this talk that there was any killing to be done. The talk was done by Bruce Evans, J. T. Canfield, and Omar LaRue.*

Q. *Do you remember the conversation of Evans, Canfield, and LaRue?*

A. *I knew it was about the killing, but do not remember the words.*

Q. *What did you go from the cabin to the river for?*

A. *Evans and Canfield went to hire a boat, and the rest went along with them.*

Q. *Did you go to the camp?*

A. *Yes.*

Q. *What was done after you got to the camp?*

A. *Neither McMillan nor I went to the camp until after the shooting.*

Q. *What camp have you reference to. Was it the Chinese camp?*

A. *Certainly.*

Q. *Did Robert McMillan do any shooting?*

A. *No.*

Q. *Was he where you could see him all the time?*

A. *Yes.*

Q. *How far were you from the Chinese camp when this shooting took place?*

A. *About two or three hundred yards.*

Q. *How far was Robert McMillan?*

A. *Near me.*

Q. *Was anyone else near you?*

A. *Bruce Evans was near, but not so close as McMillan.*

Q. *Were Canfield and LaRue near you?*

A. *No, they were not.*

Q. *After the killing, did you and McMillan go down to the boat?*

A. *We went to the Chinese camp, but not to the boat.*

Q. *What did you see when you got down to this Chinese camp?*

A. *Four or five dead Chinamen.*

Q. *Were you a witness before the grand jury that indicted these persons?*

A. *Yes sir.*

Q. *Why did you implicate Maynard, Hughes, and McMillan then, and not now?*

A. *I didn't implicate them then any more than I have now.*

Q. *Did you talk with Maynard and Hughes about the killing after returning to the cabin?*

A. *No, I did not.*

Q. *Is that all you know about the guilt or innocence of Maynard, Hughes, and McMillan?*

A. *Yes.*[1]

While O'Sullivan suggested Vaughan had changed his grand jury testimony, he did not press the point when Vaughan denied it. Indeed, O'Sullivan's questions throughout suggested he was not anxious to make any of the four reveal anything they didn't want to.

THE IRELAND-BORN O'Sullivan, then forty-six, was the first county judge for Wallowa County after it was carved out of neighboring Union County in 1887. A black and white photograph of O'Sullivan, showing him with the two other members of the first county court, or commission, is displayed in the county museum in Joseph. Looking younger than his age, with warm, sensitive eyes, O'Sullivan wears a four-inch beard without mustache or side whiskers. Although he carried the title of judge, and exercised some judicial functions, he was less a judge than the county's top political official. It is the same position held a century later by Ben Boswell.

As a politician, Judge O'Sullivan would have lacked the aura of independence normally accorded a member of the judiciary, and was more likely to be swayed by the attitudes and prejudices of his constituents. That may explain why he allowed Vaughan to get away with saying that the gang wanted only to borrow a boat from the Chinese. Moreover, O'Sullivan failed to ask the obvious: What about the gold? Indeed, there is no mention of gold anywhere in the trial documents.

During Robert McMillan's deposition, during which he gave his age as fifteen, O'Sullivan asked why he hadn't come forward sooner if he had done nothing wrong, to which the boy replied, "I was afraid to."[2] O'Sullivan didn't ask what, or who, made him afraid, or otherwise pursue the point.

The judge's lame questioning did nothing to alleviate my suspicion of a cover-up.

LEAVING THE COURTHOUSE after reading through the trial documents, I passed under a memorial arch on the northwest corner of Courthouse Square. I had passed the arch on my way into the courthouse, but hadn't paid much attention then. But I now noticed a list of names on both sides of the inside curve of the arch. The list honored the county's first settlers, beginning with William McCormack and Neil Keith, who led their cattle into the valley in 1871. Among other names that would become familiar to me in my research were those of Hiram Canfield, father of Titus Canfield; George Craig, the rancher who owned the killer's hideout and found some of the Chinese remains; Isaac Bare, a popular fiddler who wrote a song about the massacre called *Old Blue*[3]; and Seymour Horner and Alexander Findley, the fathers of the two settler historians, Harland Horner and Ross Findley. Also listed was Ben Boswell, the great-grandfather and namesake of Ben Boswell.

It wasn't until a later visit, however, that another name stood out, and astonished me, so much so that I had to walk away and return to look a second time to believe it. Midway down in a list of settlers who arrived in the Wallowa country in 1879 was a name I had overlooked before: B. E. Evans, the same Bruce Evans, leader of the gang of killers and rustlers. I

View of the Wallowa County Courthouse in Enterprise through a memorial arch dedicated to the county's earliest settlers. The plaque with the name of B. E. Evans, the leader of a gang of horse thieves accused of murdering the Chinese gold miners, is on the inside left of the arch, which was erected in 1936. (Photo by Elane Dickenson)

would learn later that Harland Horner was largely responsible for including Evans' name on the arch, which was erected in 1936. Horner wrote in his history that he was asked to provide a list of names "for the purpose of perpetuating the memory of the pioneers who migrated to, and laid the foundation for, Wallowa County, Oregon." Included among the two hundred names Horner proposed was Bruce E. Evans.[4] When the bronze plaque was cast, Bruce E. became B. E. Did someone try to make the name less obvious? No one I later talked with in the courthouse, Boswell included, could offer any explanation why Evans would be so honored. Although it was Horner who, for whatever reason, nominated Evans for the arch, it was not his responsibility alone. Others had to approve.

Every time I pass through the arch, I stare in amazement at the name, astounded that Evans, the ringleader of a gang who killed as many as thirty-four Chinese, the worst mass murder in county history, an outlaw charged with rustling and murder, who escaped at gunpoint from the county jail after subduing a deputy sheriff, and was for the rest of his life a fugitive, could be honored as a settler who "laid the foundation" for the county.

Didn't anyone care?

CHAPTER SIXTEEN

Behind the News

FOLLOWING THE INITIAL newspaper accounts in the *Lewiston Teller* of bodies being pulled from the Snake River, the massacre soon dropped from sight as a news story until the indictments and arrests were disclosed, nearly a year later.

The *Wallowa County Chieftain*, a weekly newspaper initially published in Joseph—and still published today in Enterprise—didn't run its first story on the massacre until April 19, 1888, three days after Vaughan gave his deposition and nearly a month after the indictments. An unsigned editor's note informed readers the newspaper had known of the massacre much earlier, and offered a curious explanation for not reporting it:

> *Last year about this time in an isolated locality on the Snake River fully seventy miles northeast of Joseph a number of Chinese were successfully mining on the sloping hillsides that approach the river. Late during the summer it was noted that the Chinese had disappeared and as some indications of foul play were found rumors began to circulate that the Mongolian miners had been murdered for their money supposed to be in their possession.*
>
> *The Chieftain first heard of the affair by rumor early last fall, but knowing that efforts were being made to apprehend the guilty parties if the murder proved a reality we refrained from giving the matter publicity at the time.*
>
> *Last Thursday H. K. Hughes, H. Maynard, and Robert McMillan were lodged in the jail of this place and it has become understood since, they were three of the six parties indicted by the recent Grand Jury for the murder of the Chinese miners.*[1]

The article went on to provide a description of the massacre that closely paralleled the version given by Vaughan in his deposition, suggesting the editor or reporter may have attended the deposition. The article said Vaughan, Evans, LaRue, Canfield, and McMillan went to the Chinese camp to borrow a boat to take their stolen horses across the river.

So far as anyone knows there was no plans to do the murder, or any talk about it until a small creek near the Chinese camp was reached, when Evans, Canfield, and LaRue mentioned the matter. But it is not disputed that on reaching the locality of the camp, Canfield and LaRue went above and began shooting, while Evans remained below to do his part of the dirty work. Vaughan and McMillan (a lad of only 15 years old) were near Evans, but he did none of the firing. After the Chinese, ten in number, were supposed to be killed, the bodies were thrown in the river. As night was approaching, the five individuals who were present at this unlawful and unnatural scene went back to the cabin.

The next morning Maynard and Hughes were told that the parties absent the day previous had killed some deer, and that they would go to bring them in. But as the killing of game was only a myth, Evans, Canfield, and LaRue went again to the scene of the murder, either for the purpose of removing all traces of their work, or for the gold dust the Chinese were supposed to have at their camp. We have not learned anything definitive about the action of the parties on the second day, but one rumor, which has some substantial support, is to the effect that one poor Chinaman that had not been killed, but severely wounded, had got into a boat and was working his way across the river as best he could. Shortly after the murders [sic] arrived, a wind blew the boat toward the shore where they were standing, and the Chinaman was dispatched without further ceremony.

Another rumor has it that a party of Chinese, eight in number, came up the river a few days after, and LaRue murdered them. There are also various rumors in circulation about the amount of money secured by the murderers at the Chinese camp, but no one can make a definite estimate of the plunder. It is tolerably well established however, that there was some gold, probably from one to two thousand dollars secured.[2]

The article concluded by noting that Evans, Canfield, and LaRue had fled, and that Vaughan, who had been arrested, was released after posting one thousand dollars bond. The *Chieftain's* reference to eight additional victims was the first mention of more than ten dead.

Whatever reason the newspaper had for not publicizing the crime earlier, it is doubtful it wanted to protect the investigation. Wallowa County's population in the 1880s was about three thousand, five hundred. Surely, the discovery of the murder of a single person, let alone ten, or three dozen, would quickly circulate by word of mouth. Even with ten victims, the massacre still would rank as the worst multi-death murder in the county's history. A more likely reason why the newspaper failed to report the massacre was to help protect reputations of the families of those involved. It waited until Vaughan had declared his innocence, and the innocence of the three defendants in custody, putting the blame on those who fled.

It is worth noting that small-town newspapers of this era, often just a single page or two devoted largely to advertising, came and went in a hurry. Even more than today, success depended to a considerable extent on maintaining good relations with readers and, through them, advertisers. The staff might consist of an editor, who wrote the stories and sold the ads, and maybe a helper to set type and print the papers on a hand-operated press. Editors typically would comment on the news as they wrote it, while seldom attributing the source of their information. This lack of sourcing is frustrating to anyone trying to verify facts or sort out contradictory accounts. It was to me.

Not only did the *Chieftain* delay nearly a year before reporting the murders, the April 19, 1888, edition that finally did carry the story was missing from the newspaper's files. Rick Swart, the editor of the *Chieftain*, helped me search through the musty cardboard boxes containing the newspaper's early editions, kept in the basement of the *Chieftain's* one-story Bowlby-stone building in Enterprise. Founded in 1884 in Joseph, the newspaper moved its operations to Enterprise in 1893. Whether the edition I wanted had been purposefully removed from the files, I had no way of knowing—not then. Given the newspaper's haphazard record keeping in its early years, I concluded the missing newspaper had simply been misfiled, or lost.

Once the *Chieftain* ran its story, other newspapers in Oregon and the Washington Territory picked it up, among them *The Oregonian* of Portland, the state's largest newspaper, which ran the story virtually word-for-word on an inside page on April 27, 1888. *The Oregonian* account referred to an earlier story it said it had carried on the arrest of McMillan, Maynard, and Hughes "several days ago," but I wasn't able to find it. As it was, I put my eyesight at risk reading microfilm copies of old editions for hours at a time.

ANOTHER REVEALING DOCUMENT found in the county safe was a petition signed by thirty-four prominent county residents—all men, all property owners—appealing to a Circuit Court judge to set bail to free Hughes, Maynard, and McMillan from jail because they were "illegally held."

Vaughan's April 16 deposition had set the stage for the petition. If, as he stated, Hughes and Maynard had remained at the cabin during the killings, and knew nothing about them, how could they be charged with murder? And if McMillan went along unknowingly and didn't participate in the killing, and simply watched the horses, how could justice be served by holding him? And only fifteen years old!

The handwritten petition was faded and nearly illegible. It carried no date, but would have been submitted on or before May 15, the date Judge Luther Isom responded. The petition was brief, but to the point.

> *We the undersigned citizens, householders, legal voters and taxpayers of Wallowa County, Oregon would most respectfully ask your honor to admit to bail the following parties, to wit, H. K. Hughes, H. Maynard, and Robert McMillan charged with the commission of the crime of murdering Chinamen on Snake River in said county and state. Although now the said H. K. Hughes and H. Maynard are held under the indictment of the grand jury for the commission of the above crime, it is our opinion and belief from the knowledge of the circumstances that they are wrongfully and illegally held and that our request will meet with your honorable approval, which we will ever pray.*[3]

Robert McMillan's name was not included in the original text, and was inserted later. The significance of this can only guessed at. Possibly it was an inadvertent omission, caught on a re-reading.

Among those signing the petition was James Perry Gardner, the foreman of the grand jury that returned the original indictment. How Gardner justified arguing that the defendants were illegally held under an indictment he helped produce wasn't explained. Also signing the petition was Seymour Horner, father of Harland Horner.

Judge Isom granted the petition on May 15, 1888, setting bond for the three defendants at eight hundred dollars apiece. His three-page handwritten response claimed that the depositions given by Vaughan and the defendants before Judge O'Sullivan led him to conclude their "guilt is not evident nor the proof thereof strong." In an aside, Isom mentioned that he was issuing his ruling while vacationing in Baker City, one hundred miles to the south.[4]

Maynard, Hughes, and McMillan were released. Those posting their bond included relatives and prominent members of the community. For McMillan, they included Enoch Vaughan, Frank Vaughan's father; Thomas and John Hughes, the father and brother, respectively, of Hezekiah Hughes; and William Caldwell, a witness before the grand jury. Among those posting bond for Hughes was William McCormack, one of the valley's first settlers. Maynard's bond was posted by John Hughes and family members.[5]

There is no indication any of this was reported to the Chinese government.

CHAPTER SEVENTEEN

On a Merry-Go-Round

NOT EVERYONE IN Wallowa County chose to ignore or downplay the significance of the crime.

James Slater, a former U.S. Senator, voiced his concern in a letter to the U.S. Attorney for Oregon, L. L. McArthur, on April 24, 1888. Slater sought federal assistance to help investigate "a most daring outrage on a camp of unoffending Chinamen who were mining on Snake River."[1] Slater served in the U.S. Senate from Oregon from 1879 to 1885 and, according to one account, introduced a bill in 1879 to allow Chinese to live and travel in the United States, but not work—the bill didn't pass.[2]

In his two-page typewritten letter, found in the National Archives, Slater wrote about the murders as if McArthur might not have heard of them, and, indeed, he may not have. Slater told him two Chinese were killed and probably "many more." He was apparently referring to the bodies found in Hells Canyon by George Craig, but he made no mention of the bodies recovered at Lewiston ten months earlier, suggesting the connection of those bodies to the massacre wasn't yet known in Wallowa County.

Slater identified Evans, Canfield, and LaRue as "the ringleaders" of a gang that robbed the Chinese of "$5,000 or $10,000 in gold dust." The others, he wrote, were in jail, except for Vaughan, who had turned state's evidence.

> *Frank Vaughan testified before the grand jury and gave the whole matter away. The feeling here is quite intense against the accused and a general desire is expressed that all the parties should be brought to punishment, but the county is not in a condition to push the prosecution ... I regard the matter in a most serious light and feel sure that if the matter be laid before the proper authority the whole power of the government will be brought to bear to bring the guilty to justice.*[3]

Slater urged McArthur to convince Washington to send men and resources to track down Evans, Canfield, and LaRue, who "are at large and out of the state." His estimate of the value of gold taken from the Chinese miners must have come from Vaughan, as he had no basis for making his own estimate.

Not surprisingly, Slater's request for federal help fell on deaf ears, just as had the Chinese legation's appeal weeks earlier. His letter prompted an exchange of meaningless correspondence that would be comical, were the situation not so tragic.

U.S. Attorney McArthur figuratively threw up his hands and forwarded Slater's letter on April 28 to both U.S. Attorney General A. H. Garland and Secretary of State Bayard "in the hope that you may be able to devise some means of assisting the local authorities ... in bringing the guilty men to justice."[4]

Garland replied on May 14 that the government didn't have authority to become involved in the case, and, in any event, lacked the funds to assist in tracking down the suspects who fled.[5]

Bayard's office, for its part, forwarded Slater's letter to the Chinese legation on May 15, informing Minister Chang that the federal government was powerless to intervene in a state matter. Incredibly, he suggested the Chinese themselves might provide the help Slater was seeking for local authorities.

> *It seems probable that much aid in the indicated direction might be rendered to the authorities of the State of Oregon having jurisdiction in the premises, by the Chinese consul at San Francisco, who has heretofore interested himself in tracing out the authors of this grievous crime and endeavoring to procure their trial and conviction.*
>
> *The crime having been committed against the laws and peace of Oregon, and the indictment against certain of the alleged murderers having been found by the criminal courts of that state, there is not present reason for federal jurisdiction in the premises, or for interference to procure testimony on the part of the judicial officers of the United States. The Chinese consulate at San Francisco and his agents, with the witnesses to the facts mentioned in your previous note, will, I am sure, be afforded every courtesy and facility by the authorities of the state of Oregon, of whose energetic disposition to take advantage of every opportunity to further the ends of justice, Senator Slater's letter affords gratifying proof.*[6]

How the Chinese might provide the resources to pursue the killers in a climate of anti-Chinese feeling, and under what authority, wasn't addressed.

And, of course, the Sam Yup Company had already dispatched Lee Loi, who had hired Vincent, who proved of little help. But the letter did contain important information for the Chinese. It was apparently the first they had heard of the arrests.

Chang sent a courteous reply on May 20, expressing "my hearty thanks for the information … I shall send a copy of the same without delay to the consul-general at San Francisco, and direct him to take such action in the matter as is within his power to aid the local authorities in discovering and bringing to punishment the wicked men who perpetrated the murder."[7]

Chang's brief May 20 reply was the last mention of the massacre by the Chinese I could find in the National Archives.

THE CHINESE by this time had given up on Vincent. The consulate's detailed letter to Bayard on February 16, 1888, referred to unanswered queries sent to Vincent over several months. Vincent evidently had stopped investigating because he wasn't any longer being paid, although Gerald Tucker, the former Forest Service employee, said in his unattributed account that incent was offered a reward of one thousand dollars. For his part, Vincent said he was paid two hundred dollars, in itself a not insignificant sum. However, there was nothing in the National Archives correspondence to suggest he conducted anything more than a cursory investigation.

Vincent's final communication in the National Archives was dated April 14, 1888, and was sent in response to a query from Idaho's territorial governor, Edward Stevenson, who, in turn, was following up on Secretary of State Bayard's request for information. By this time, Vincent had lost whatever contact he had with the investigation. He seemed unaware of the recent major developments: the grand jury indictment handed down three weeks earlier in Joseph, Frank Vaughan's confession, and the arrest of several members of the Evans gang. Instead, he appealed to Governor Stevenson for money to pursue clues he claimed to have uncovered, while rehashing what he had already told the Chinese he had done, or not done.

[U]ntil lately I have been unable to find much out, and not being able in a monetary point to go where I would wish to, to trace up the matter, it has rested.

There has never been any reward offered and as far as my six weeks trial in hunting before with one man, the Chinamen paid me two hundred dollars, and that, out of their own pockets.

I have received within the past two weeks some information which strikes strongly on the case. The letter to a friend of mine is written by a man from Joseph, Oregon and he says he thinks he can find out all about the murder and thinks he can find four of the murderers if he is paid enough; and he has certain proof he can bring to bear on the case, but I have not answered the letter as yet, as I expected to hear from the China Co. [sic] of San Francisco.

There has never been any reward offered and the most of us here are too poor to work for glory, in tracing up such brutal murders.[8]

There's no way to reconcile the difference between the one thousand dollars the Chinese were said to have offered Vincent as a reward, and the two hundred dollars Vincent said he received. With his large home, wheat fields, and prestigious marriage, it is difficult to imagine Vincent was, in any event, desperate for money.

Stevenson forwarded Vincent's letter to Bayard on April 19, saying that since the crime had been committed in Oregon, his hands were tied. But in a statement that smacked of hollow bluster, the governor said: "If this murder had been committed in this territory by its citizens, I should have offered a large reward for the apprehension and conviction of the murderers. But as the crime was done in an adjoining state, I have no jurisdiction."[9]

Stevenson's own record with respect to the territory's Chinese was mixed. He had issued a proclamation on April 27, 1886, warning against threatened anti-Chinese violence in the Idaho Territory, and pledging equal protection of the laws for Chinese. On the other hand, he was quoted in official correspondence with Secretary of State Bayard on August 2, 1886, as characterizing the Chinese in derogatory terms and expressing hope that "the day is not far off when Congress will relieve us of their presence."[10]

CHAPTER EIGHTEEN

Claims for Corpses

CHINA'S GOVERNMENT, recognizing the unlikely prospect that anyone would be punished for crimes against the Chinese, including murder, pressed its efforts for financial compensation.[1]

Prior to departing Washington for health reasons, the head of the Chinese legation, Cheng Tsao Ju, sent Secretary of State Bayard a new list of claims for crimes, including the twenty-eight Chinese murdered at Rock Springs. Congress had previously settled property claims from Rock Springs, but provided nothing for the families of the victims.

Cheng's successor, Chang Yen Hoon, updated the list on March 3, 1888, citing forty murders, not counting those along the Snake River in Hells Canyon. To satisfy the claims, Chang sought 346,619.75 dollars in compensation, of which one hundred thousand dollars was indemnification for those killed—computed at two thousand, five hundred dollars per death.

Chang forwarded the updated list following a meeting with Bayard. His cover letter suggested that the meeting had bogged down in haggling over whether the claims for property damage should include the uncollected debts of merchants forced out of business by the Rock Springs violence. The complete list follows. It reveals the extent of the crimes occurring within the span of a few years, and includes notations that the legation had previously notified Bayard's office of most of the incidents. While Chang mentioned the Snake River killings in passing, the Rock Springs violence continued to evoke his major concern.

It will be noted that the statement includes a claim on account of the twenty-eight lives lost at the Rock Springs riot in 1885. When the estimate for property losses was sent to you with the note of my predecessor of November 30, 1885, it was hoped that due punishment would be inflicted upon the wicked men who so cruelly murdered the Chinese subjects in that horrible affair, and thus their relatives would have the satisfaction of knowing that some atonement had been made, and for which punishment I have in my notes made repeated requests. But since not a single one of the murderers has been punished, it seems highly just that some compensation should be made to the families of the unfortunate men, and I know so well your high sense of justice and kindness of heart that I am satisfied you will recognize this claim as well founded.

With sentiments of the highest regard, I remain ...
Chang Yen Hoon

STATEMENT OF CLAIMS
1. Property Losses

In note of April 5, 1886:

Squak Valley, Washington Territory	$535.65
Coal Creek Mine, Washington Territory	4,054.88
Almy, Wyoming Territory	6,064.70

In note of August 11, 1886:

Anaconda, Montana Territory	3,000.00

In note of February 19, 1887:

Tacoma, Washington Territory—

Losses in the town	106,919.60
Losses in the vicinity	7,530.65

In note of February 19, 1887:

Seattle, Washington Territory—

Losses as stated in inclosure [sic] accompanying note	$143,851.87	
Deducting claims based upon uncollected debts, per statement attached hereto	35,337.60	
There remains in the Seattle claim		108,514.27

In note of February 25, 1887:

Juneau, Alaska Territory. No detailed estimate of losses yet filed. About 100 Chinese were expelled. Estimating $100 each for property losses and expenses of journey to San Francisco and elsewhere would amount to — 10,000.00

In note of February 15, 1886:

A statement of riots at Bloomfield, Redding, Boulder Creek, Eureka, And other towns in California, involving murder, arson, robbery, and expulsion, but no estimates. Also a statement that near 100,000 Chinese had been driven from their homes.

Total of property losses, as estimated — 246,619.75

II.—Loss of lives

In note of November 30, 1885:

    Rock Springs, Wyoming Territory. Number of lives lost in riot,

        besides 16 wounded   28

In note of April 5, 1886:

    Squak Valley, Washington Territory. Number of lives

        lost (and 4 Wounded)   3

    Orofino, Idaho Territory.[2] Number of lives lost   5

In note of August 11, 1886:

    Anaconda, Montana Territory. Number of lives lost   4

In note of February 16, 1888:

    Snake River, Oregon. Number of lives reported lost   10

If the Snake River murders are omitted, of which no accurate information is yet received, there remain forty lives of Chinese by riots and violence for which no compensation has yet been made. If the indemnity paid by Spain to the United States in the Virginius case is accepted, $2,500 as the lowest sum, there would result a claim for $100,000. Add as above, property losses, $246,619.75; grand total, $346,619.75.[3]

IN SEEKING COMPENSATION, Chang wasn't without negotiating leverage. He knew of the American desire for a new immigration treaty to replace the 1882 Exclusion Act, due to expire in 1892. President Cleveland wanted to both extend and toughen its terms. With a presidential election looming in 1888, Cleveland, a Democrat, hoped a more restrictive treaty would improve his standing with voters in the four western states of California, Oregon, Colorado, and Nevada. At the same time, China's Qing rulers didn't want to overplay their hand. They also favored additional restrictions on emigration, both to quell anti-American feeling in China and to maintain good relations with Washington. Chang proposed the wording the Chinese wanted in a new treaty, including the right of laborers to return to the United States following visits home.

Bayard's response to Chang on March 7, 1888, acknowledged the link between the treaty and the compensation issue. He accepted the Chinese request for the right of return, but sought to narrow it by setting a time limit. He also tried to wriggle out of responsibility for the Rock Springs massacre.

Sir: I had the honor to receive, on the 5th instant, your note of the 3d instant, accompanied by a full statement of the pecuniary estimate of all the losses in property and injuries to person suffered by Chinese subjects throughout the United States in remote and unsettled localities at the hands of lawless and cruel men.

I have carefully considered the amended draughts of the proposed articles of the treaty and shall accept the modifications as they appear in the manuscript sent by you, asking, however, that a reasonable limitation upon the period of their voluntary absence from the United States shall be fixed within which Chinese subjects must avail themselves of the right to return to the United States.

The tragedy at Rock Springs in 1885 should, however, be considered as having been deliberately closed as between the two governments, and I am not wholly without hope that the hand of justice may yet reach the perpetrators of those crimes, none of whom, however were citizens of the United States.

You will comprehend the obvious expediency of concluding the proposed convention at the earliest possible day.[4]

CHAPTER NINETEEN

A Kind of Trial

THERE IS NOTHING to indicate that the one-story stucco and brick building at the corner of West Main and First streets in Enterprise once housed a courtroom where, in the closing days of August, 1888, a murder trial was held for Hiram Maynard, Robert McMillan, and Hezekiah Hughes.

The courtroom is gone. Indeed, the building's entire second story is missing, removed in a 1966 renovation. What remains of the original building was, the last time I saw it, painted a robin's egg blue, with a flat, brown-shingled roof overlapping the walls, giving it a kind of bizarre South Pacific islands look.

Far more is known about the building and its history than about the trial held inside. Constructed by the Inland City Mercantile and Milling Company in 1888, it was the first office building in Enterprise. A bank occupied the ground floor, with the second floor leased to Wallowa County when voters moved the county seat from Joseph to Enterprise in 1888. The

A photo taken in 1900 of the building where the 1888 trial was held. This was before the remodeling that removed the second floor. (Courtesy of the Wallowa County Museum in Joseph)

second floor housed the courtroom and the sheriff's office, plus offices for the county clerk, county judge, and county assessor.[1] As an incentive for voters to approve the move to Enterprise, the building owners agreed in advance to charge the county a dollar a year, and also committed to building a jail nearby.

The courtroom was in use for twenty years. Courtroom windows offered an unobstructed view of the Wallowa Mountains to the south, across a wide expanse of lush farmland and pasture. I imagined the defendants at the murder trial sitting smugly at the defense table, looking out toward the farms and mountains, confident they would soon be free to return to them.

CHARLOTTE McIVER'S CHANCE discovery of the long-forgotten documents in the courthouse safe provided the first substantive information in many years about the trial. Previously, the only known record of the trial was a brief notation in the Circuit Court docket, listing the trial date, the names of the defendants, and the verdict. But no detail of the trial itself had been known to exist, although Horner's unpublished county history, which surfaced only in recent years, revealed he had had access to the trial documents.

Curiously, I could not find a single newspaper account of the trial proceedings. It is difficult to believe the *Chieftain* didn't cover the trial, not only because of the large number of victims, and the brutality of the crime, but also because it was the county's first murder trial. For today's media, the prominence of some of those involved would have been reason alone to cover the trial. But in 1888, a family's status and the threat of public scandal might well have been a reason *not* to cover the trial. Still, it seems improbable that having reported the indictments and arrests, the *Chieftain* wouldn't have at least followed up with the trial verdict.

I can't prove beyond doubt that the *Chieftain* didn't report the trial. As noted earlier, editions from that period were missing from the newspaper's haphazard early files. Nevertheless, since I also didn't find a trial story in the files of *The Oregonian*, which relied on the *Chieftain* for its massacre coverage, I took this as evidence that the *Chieftain* hadn't reported the outcome. From today's perspective, I can say the editors of *The Oregonian* were remiss in not sending a reporter from Portland. However, the newspaper was then quite small, often just four pages. Considering the tenor of the times, the editors might well have concluded that the trial wasn't worth the expense of a sending one of their few reporters on a long trip over primitive roads to the far northeastern corner of the state. Editors of the day didn't require focus groups to tell them readers weren't interested in certain subjects. Assuming I'm correct that the *Chieftain* didn't cover the trial, it proved a key step in the cover-up that appeared already very much underway.

IT WASN'T ONLY newspapers that ignored the trial. I couldn't find any mention of the actual trial or the outcome in the National Archives' correspondence, neither incoming nor outgoing. Nor was there anything to indicate the Chinese ever learned of the verdict. China's legation had been informed of the arrests, but apparently didn't inquire about the trial— at least not to the State Department. Perhaps legation officials found out from other sources, or perhaps they had simply given up. At the time, the Chinese were unaware of the full scope of the massacre. And a major reason they remained unaware was that authorities in Wallowa County, whether purposefully or out of disinterest, kept important details of the massacre from leaking out of the county.

The trial was also virtually ignored in the two settler accounts. Findley didn't mention it at all. Improbable as it seems, he appeared oblivious there even was a trial.

> *It was believed that the boys were led into committing the murders by older and evil-minded leaders who were responsible for the crime, and as none of these men were ever apprehended or punished, the school boys were never prosecuted. None of these boys had taken any part in the actual killing of the Chinese.*[2]

In his account, Horner acknowledged a trial, but dismissed it in six words after writing that LaRue, Evans, and Canfield had fled the area. "Their companions were tried and acquitted."[3]

The trial extended over two days, on August 30 and 31 of 1888, or so I at first thought. Among the documents in the safe were fifteen subpoenas for witnesses; three pages of abbreviated trial proceedings, each with the notation "journal entry," and the verdict. The judge is not identified in these documents, but he was Circuit Judge Luther Isom, who had earlier approved releasing the defendants on bond, saying evidence against them appeared weak.

The journal entries are handwritten. The first, a one-page entry, simply notes that "on this day" Hughes, Maynard, and McMillan entered pleas of not guilty to charges of murder. It lists the defense attorneys as Ivanhoe & Smith, M. L. Olmstead, Pipes and Gowan, and the district attorney as J. L. Rand. But it provides no substantive information about the trial itself.

The second journal entry is two pages and covers the second day of the trial. It is notable mostly for the lack of information it provides.

Now on this day this cause came to be herd [sic] on the trial of the defts [defendants] Hyram [sic] Maynard, Hezekiah Hughes indicted under the name of Carl Hughes, and Robert McMillan for the crime of murder appearing by J. L. Rand and the defts in person as well as by the same attys [attorneys] as of yesterday whereupon the same jurors as of yesterday proceeded to hear further testimony for the state and for the defts and after hearing the argument of counsel of the state and for the defts and the instructions of the court they retired to deliberate upon their verdict and after deliberation they returned the following verdict.[4]

The word "verdict" was written vertically down the page, evidently to leave space for the actual verdict. The account continued on a second page.

Whereupon the court ordered the defts to be discharged from further custody and that their indict [sic] asking of bail be ... and that their sureties on the undertaking towit [sic]... be released from further liability on their said several undertakings.[5]

The ellipses are in the document. There are also blank spaces on the second page, evidently for information to be inserted later. The account must have been written in advance, perhaps anticipating an innocent verdict. There was another possible explanation; the randomness of the writing, the spelling errors, abbreviations, frequent cross-outs, and the lack of a date, suggested to me that the pages were sketchy drafts for a trial record to be entered into a court journal later. But if there was such a journal, it was not among the documents in the safe, nor was it found elsewhere in the county clerk's office.

Some of the fifteen subpoenaed witnesses presumably testified. Curiously, all but one are identified as prosecution witnesses, including Frank Vaughan and the rancher, George Craig. Also listed as prosecution witnesses are William Maynard, Hiram Maynard's father, and Seymour Horner, one of the thirty-four taxpayers who had claimed in the petition to Judge Isom that the defendants were illegally held. Seeing Vaughan's and Horner's names among the prosecution witnesses was puzzling, since they were already on record arguing the innocence of the defendants. All of the witnesses were reimbursed for their court appearances—Vaughan received ten dollars and twenty cents.[6]

IN HIS TESTIMONY, Vaughan surely told the same story as in his April 16 deposition, placing all the blame for the massacre on Evans, Canfield and LaRue, while absolving the others of guilt. He would have testified that Maynard and Hughes took no part in the massacre because they stayed behind at the cabin, while McMillan simply watched the horses. If anyone asked the motive for the murders, Vaughan would have avoided any mention of gold, offering the same explanation as before, that Evans and the other killers became enraged when the Chinese refused to lend them their boat.

We don't know whether District Attorney Rand voiced any skepticism about Vaughan's account, or pressed him on whether the killers weren't really after the gold. Of course, if Vaughan had been asked that question, and answered in the affirmative, he no doubt would have faced such crucial follow-up questions as, How much gold? Who took it? Where was it? Such an avenue of inquiry might have proved embarrassing to Vaughan, as well as the others. It could have implicated the defendants in a different crime: robbery. Or, perhaps there were other reasons for not mentioning the gold. There is also no way of knowing whether Rand, or anyone else, asked about other victims beyond the ten named in the indictment.

The documents in the safe also included the verdict, written on a separate piece of paper:

In the Circuit Court of the State of Oregon for the County of Wallowa
The State of Oregon vs Hyram [sic] Maynard and Robert McMillan

and Hezikiah [sic] Hughes indicted under the name of Carl Hughes—
implicated with J. T. Canfield, Bruce Evans, and C. O. Larue [sic],
defendants.

We the jury in the above entitled action find the defendants Hyram
Maynard, Robert McMillan, and Hezekiah Hughes—Not Guilty.
William Green, Foreman[7]

THERE IS YET another account of the trial, however brief. Years later, George Craig, who, aside from Vaughan, knew more about the massacre than any other witness, gave his recollection to an interviewer. It was Craig, of course, who, with his son, had found some of the bodies in Hells Canyon. And it was Craig who owned the old Douglas cabin used by Evans' gang as a hideout. No doubt Craig knew Evans and Canfield well—his ranch was in the same general area on Pine Creek, making them near neighbors. The notes from the interview, conducted on March 2, 1936 by an unnamed researcher for the Works Progress Administration, the Depression-era jobs program, are in the University of Oregon library. David Stratton first made use of them in his account of the massacre.

Written in long hand, the five-page interview unfortunately does not include direct quotes, and not all of it is legible. The interviewer wrote that "George Craig was present at the trial and heard every bit of it."[8] Craig seemed to accept Vaughan's version of the massacre—that the killing was triggered by an argument with the Chinese over their boat. But he appeared confused as to who was where during the shooting. He said Vaughan remained behind at the cabin, even though Vaughan said in his deposition that he accompanied the killers to the Chinese camp, testimony he surely repeated at the trial. It is possible the interviewer confused the names; it is also possible Craig's memory of the trial was fuzzy. At the time of the interview, he was eighty-one, and nearly fifty years had elapsed. But it is also not out of the question that Craig decided to go along with a community-wide whitewash of Vaughan's role.

As to the number of victims, the interviewer wrote that Craig was adamant that many more than ten Chinese were murdered. And he offered yet another version of the massacre, suggesting that all of the victims were killed in a single attack at a single location.

The Chinamen were thirty-one in number and all of them were murdered ... These Chinamen resided in a small cove, which was surrounded by the murderers who shot the Chinamen down with long-range rifles. The white men killed thirty of the Chinese and broke the arm of another. This wounded Chinaman ran to the Snake River and got into a small skiff, but the murderers pursued him and killed him with rocks. The murderers threw all of the bodies of the murdered Chinamen into the Snake River and for years afterward the carcasses of the victims were found along its banks. George Craig himself buried several of the bodies.[9]

In his 1983 article about the massacre, Stratton quoted Craig as saying in a separate newspaper interview that the trial verdict was a foregone conclusion because the victims were Chinese: "I guess if they had killed thirty-one white men something would have been done about it, but none of the jury knew the Chinamen or cared much about it, so they turned the men loose."[10] Stratton attributed the quote to an undated interview with Craig by a former *Oregon Journal* newspaper columnist, Fred Lockley. The same quote, with the same attribution to Lockley, had appeared in Gerald Tucker's 1961 magazine article. Tucker had also quoted Craig from an unattributed interview on March 2, 1936, which was the date of the WPA interview, and presumably was one and the same.

Hughes, Maynard, Vaughan, and McMillan turned state's evidence and told the story on the witness stand, and I was present at the trial and heard every bit of it because I was interested to know. I knew all of them except LaRue, and was curious to know what the facts were.

Hughes and Maynard were sent one up the river and one down the river to see that nobody came. That was the first thing that was done. Vaughan was left in the house to get dinner and Bob McMillan held the horses and watched them kill the Chinamen.

Carcasses of these Chinamen were found for years after this along the river. I have buried several of the carcasses myself.[11]

Assuming the information did come from the WPA interview, Tucker was attributing to Craig direct quotes from comments that had only been paraphrased by the interviewer.

I was unable to locate a Lockley interview. However, I did find in the Wallowa County Museum a column with much the same information, written on August 4, 1966, by Ben Weathers, the then-publisher of the *Wallowa County Chieftain*. Weathers, who knew Craig, also paraphrased Craig's comments rather than putting them in quotation marks. He attributed much of the information in his column to Craig's son, Frazier. He said the Craigs, father and son, had found "a number of skeletons along the bank of the river and on sand bars."

> *Frazier was eleven or twelve and told me of finding a cache of flour, rice, and tobacco hidden in the rocks near the mouth of a little stream near Upper Deep Creek and he and his dad also found where the killers had burned part of their victims' clothing, and in the ashes, Frazier found a good sized nugget and some buttons and other trinkets.*[12]

Writing of the 1888 trial, Weathers went on to say: "Chinamen were not held in very high esteem in those days and it is doubtful any of the jurymen ever had any qualms after turning the killers loose. Had it been white men who were the victims, no doubt, it would have been a different story."[13] Weather's comment suggests that the almost identical comment on the injustice of the verdict that was widely attributed to Craig, actually originated with Weathers. Weathers, like Findley before him, wrote of the massacre without mentioning the names of those involved.

ALTHOUGH THE DOCUMENTS from the safe made references to a trial journal, I was unable for a long while to locate the journal or anyone with knowledge of one. But I kept asking, believing the journal might include actual trial testimony.

CHAPTER TWENTY

Wanted: Horse Thieves

THERE WAS STILL the matter of the whereabouts of Evans, Canfield, and LaRue, who had fled Wallowa County. The only indication anyone so much as thought about pursuing them was the written appeal from the former U.S. senator, James Slater, seeking federal help to track them down. But when the government brushed off the appeal, Slater apparently dropped the matter.

In addition to being charged with murder, Evans and Canfield also were wanted on rustling charges resulting from the theft of the horses entrusted to Evans by the rancher, Fred Nodine. Records of this case were also found in the county safe, no doubt placed there by whoever stashed the murder trial records.

In contrast to the spotty information on the massacre, I was surprised to find the records on the rustling case had been maintained in meticulous detail. An example was this handwritten account by Justice of the Peace J. J. Stanley of Evans' arrest on May 30, 1877, and Evans' subsequent court appearances after being charged with "altering and defacing" brands on six horses.

> *May 23. Information filed and warrant issued and placed in the hands of Thomas Humphrey for the arrest of the said Bruce Evans.*
>
> *May 30. The defendant brought before me and informed of the charge against him. He then asked for time to procure counsel and witnesses. Examination set for 10 o'clock of the 31st.*
>
> *May 31. Subpoenas for John Nodine, A. Beckelheimer, William Martin, William Newby, George Ferguson, O. C. Oleson and T. Humphrey as witnesses issued on behalf of the state.*
>
> *May 31. Subpoenas for Omer Larue [sic] and Robert McMillan as witnesses on behalf of the defendant.*
>
> *May 31. Examination opened and the following witnesses sworn in on behalf of the state [sic] William Martin, J. A. McAdams, William Newby, O. C. Olesen and George Ferguson. The examinations on behalf of the state closed, and the defendant was informed that it is his right to make a statement ... The defendant waived his right to make*

[sic] statement and it appearing from the evidence that the defendant has committed the crime of altering and defacing a brand as charged in the information on file, he is held to answer the same in the sum of two thousand dollars.[1]

The rustling case and the massacre were inextricably linked. The massacre started on May 25, two days after an arrest warrant had been issued for Evans on May 23, and five days before his arrest on May 30. Vaughan's faked attempt to serve Evans with a subpoena on May 11—to give evidence in the rustling case against Canfield—would have alerted Evans that authorities were closing in.

When arrested, Evans lacked the money to post his bond, set at two thousand dollars, even though he earlier had helped Canfield with his bail following his arrest on May 10. But Canfield's bail had been set lower, at eight hundred dollars. Evans may have been considered a greater flight risk, although, as it turned out, Canfield proved no less a risk. It may also have been indicative of Evans' fading fortunes that no one stepped forward on his behalf to post bond.

Findley wrote in his history that Evans' escape from custody on June 15 was planned by other gang members, who had slipped him a message advising "that at a certain hour he would find a loaded revolver in the outdoor toilet and a saddled horse would be waiting at the intersection of a certain street."[2] Other gang members may have arranged his escape because they were afraid he would implicate them in the massacre, which county authorities still hadn't discovered. Or they may have freed him to get their share of the stolen gold. Or, out of comradery.

Findley linked Evans' escape to the supposed confession of one of the younger gang members to the murders. But Findley had to have been mistaken. Vaughan's confession, and the grand jury indictments, were still months away. Moreover, Findley said the escape occurred six months after the murders, when court records revealed it was only two weeks later.

Horner, who provided additional details of the escape, didn't link Evans' flight to a confession. He named Vaughan and Hughes as the gang members who helped Evans escape, adding the detail that not one, but two, revolvers were stashed in the outhouse.

And when Evans stepped out, he had a revolver in each hand and covered [deputy Thomas] Humphreys, and told him to take a walk, which he did. Two revolvers having been cached in the toilet for Evans, supposed to have been put there by Carl [Hezekiah] Hughes. And Evans ran and jumped on a horse tied to a hitching rack close by, placed there for him by some of his bunch, supposedly by Frank Vaughan, and rode off in a dead run. When Evans told Humphreys to take a walk, he told him not to follow him. For if he did, he would be killed.[3]

Vaughan also had reason to be nervous prior to the massacre. Even though he had been entrusted by Justice of the Peace J. J. Stanley to serve a subpoena on Evans on May 11, Vaughan himself was served with a subpoena the following day, on May 12, ordering him to appear at the hearing for Canfield, scheduled for May 16.

Clearly, the sheriff of Wallowa County, Robert Coshow, was deconstructing, bit by bit, the Evans gang and its rustling activities, although, as the days went by, he remained oblivious to the blood spilled in Hells Canyon. He personally served the subpoenas on LaRue and McMillan on May 31 directing them to appear as defense witnesses for Evans. The sheriff found them nearby, as he sought reimbursement for just four miles of travel. Why Evans would pick them as defense witnesses, since they had joined him in the massacre, is curious. Either of them, especially fifteen-year-old McMillan, might panic and talk, although there is no evidence either did so.

One can only speculate as to the emotions of LaRue and McMillan when the sheriff approached with the subpoenas: surprise, remorse, fear? Perhaps all three. But after learning that the subpoenas related not to murder, but to rustling, their worry may have subsided. They appeared at the May 31 hearing for Evans, as county court records show each was paid one dollar and seventy cents in witness fees. But LaRue probably didn't wait long before he fled. Horner wrote he left the county soon after the massacre.

Evans, however, stuck around for a time after escaping from jail, although he kept away from his ranch and his family on Pine Creek. Horner reported that Evans hid out along the Imnaha River, supported by other gang members and their relatives, until the massacre was finally discovered by Oregon authorities. Horner didn't say whether Evans was in contact with his wife and children.

When Evans got away, he went to Imnaha and camped in the brush by a small spring creek on the west side of the river, opposite Hugh McMillan's place [sic] who was father of Robert McMillan, and the family carried provisions for him for several weeks to this camp. From there he had a full view of the Imnaha road and up and down the river for a ways. During this time, Vaughan and some others of the bunch kept McMillan posted on what was going on and McMillan through his daughter, Janie, who carried food to Evans in his camp, would tell Evans. There were a few, not of the bunch, were on the lookout for Evans. And a rancher and stockman who lived on Big Sheep Creek while hunting one day, too close to Evans' hideout, saw Evans rise up, laid his gun across a log, told the man to take a walk and hurry about it. So that night Evans changed his camp. When it was learned about the killing of the Chinamen, Evans skipped for parts unknown.[4]

Canfield also didn't flee immediately.

For several weeks, before Canfield skipped, he went to where his parents had squatted on a place on Camp Creek at the junction of it and Trail Creek. Their cabin was about three hundred yards up Camp Creek. And Canfield piled up some stones in a gap in a cliff, where he had a good view of the trail and road on Trail Creek and slept there. Stockmen and officers could have rode along the trail above him within fifty feet and not noticed his layout. His parents and sister, Minnie, prepared his meals for him.[5]

It makes no sense to me that Evans and Canfield would remain in Wallowa County following the massacre—unless they were hoping for an opportunity to dig up the buried gold. Even though the murders hadn't yet been discovered in the county, rustling was a serious crime. Moreover, Evans was a fugitive, facing a possible lengthy prison sentence if apprehended. On August 25, 1887, a Circuit Court grand jury indicted both Evans and Canfield for a second time on the brand-altering charge. Judge Isom forfeited Canfield's bail, noting he had failed on three occasions to appear in court to answer the rustling charge. By this time, Canfield and Evans had fled, with or without the gold.

It was not until the following March that the grand jury indicted Evans, Canfield, LaRue, and the others for murder. After Maynard, McMillan, and Hughes were declared innocent in the 1888 trial, the court continued the murder charges against Evans, Canfield, and LaRue, charges for which they were never held to account.

With Evans gone, somebody had to take care of his horses. That job fell to Deputy Humphreys, who had stared down the barrel of Evans' gun. The county paid him sixty-nine dollars to care for Evans' herd.

CHAPTER TWENTY-ONE

Tightening the Screws

ON SEPTEMBER 1, 1888, the same day the jury in Enterprise returned its not guilty verdict for Hughes, Maynard, and McMillan, the U.S. Senate ratified a new immigration treaty with China, known as the Bayard-Chang Treaty.

As written, the new treaty extended the immigration ban against Chinese laborers for another twenty years. It also made it more difficult for Chinese to return to the U.S. if they left for visits home. They could reenter only if they could prove ownership of at least one thousand dollars in assets, or had immediate family in the United States, which few did, since most laborers had left their families in China. In a trade-off benefiting China, the treaty included the much sought-after compensation package for property losses and murders. Both governments seemed pleased.

However, what appeared to be an amicable outcome quickly deteriorated when the Qing dynasty rulers delayed ratifying the treaty to address widespread opposition to the accord in Guangdong Province. The delay was misinterpreted in Washington as a rejection of the treaty, prompting Congress to fly into a legislative rage. Representative William Scott, a leading Democrat from Pennsylvania and friend of President Cleveland, drafted a bill known as the Scott Act that was aimed at preventing Chinese from returning to American shores under any circumstances.[1]

The House approved the Scott Act unanimously; the Senate followed suit with only three dissenting votes. Senator John Mitchell, an Oregon Republican, said his "only criticism" was that the legislation failed to go far enough—he had supported the ouster of Portland's Chinese during the 1886 agitation.[2] News accounts of the debate over the Scott Act quoted Mitchell as arguing that "If he had his will he would make exclusion apply not only to the four hundred million Chinamen in China, but to those now in the United States." Senator Arthur Gorman of Maryland tried to stem the anti-Chinese tide after learning from the State Department that the Chinese were merely delaying action on the treaty, not rejecting it. The Senate's hasty and wrong-headed response, he predicted, would backfire.

*We are all united in restricting Chinese immigration, and I do not
believe that in this contest there is any advantage on either side. If we
go on in face of the information which we have received today, we will
destroy our own trade with China and make it impossible for this great
nation ... to have an outlet in China for its products, and close a door
which during years past we have tried by fleets and special ministers to
keep open.*[3]

Extending over several days, the debate disintegrated at times into an
acrimonious blame game over which political party was responsible for
Chinese immigration in the first place. Senator James George, a Mississippi
Democrat, blamed the Republicans, while complaining that his own
credibility had been unfairly attacked by Mitchell, who had brought up
George's past as a slaveholder.[4]

Over diplomatic protests from the Chinese, and even objections by
Secretary of State Bayard, President Cleveland signed the bill on October
1, 1888. Its immediate result was to bar about twenty thousand workers
temporarily in China, even though they held valid exit visas for return to the
United States. As many as six hundred U.S.-bound Chinese were stranded at
sea, unable to complete their voyage.[5] The legislation soured U.S.-Chinese
relations for decades and wasn't fully repealed until 1943.

President Cleveland had hoped by taking a hard stance against the
Chinese he could win the electoral votes of California, Oregon, Nevada,
and Colorado in the 1888 election. But his gamble failed; he lost all four
states, and the election, to Benjamin Harrison.

The Chinese, angered by the Scott Act, never ratified the Bayard-Chang
Treaty. But they did receive the compensation package. On October 19,
1888, Acting Secretary of State G. L. Rives notified Chang, then out of the
country, that Congress had approved much of what he sought.

*I have the pleasure to inform you that the President today approved
an act, recently passed by the Congress, entitled "An Act making
appropriations to supply deficiencies in the appropriation for the
fiscal year ending June 30, 1888, and for other purposes," in which
an appropriation is made, "to pay, out of humane consideration and
without reference to the question of liability therefore, the sum of two
hundred and seventy-six thousand, six hundred and nineteen dollars*

and seventy-five cents to the Chinese government as full indemnity for all losses and injuries sustained by Chinese subjects within the United States and the lands of residents thereof."

It affords me great satisfaction to acquaint you with this generous provision on the part of the government of the United States, to relieve the unfortunate subjects of his majesty the Emperor of China, who have suffered in their persons and property at the hands of evil-doers, whose acts can in no wise be imparted to the government or to the right-minded people of the United States, however much they call for sincere and sorrowful regret and appeal—and not in vain—to alleviate the distressed condition of those so injured by acts of lawlessness.[6]

Rives chose to overlook the fact that the Chinese had not included in its claim any compensation for the Hells Canyon massacre. Nonetheless, the Chinese appeared satisfied.

On receiving the news, Chang must have felt considerable relief—even though the amount was seventy thousand dollars less than requested. He had been accused in China of mishandling the treaty negotiations, and his house in Guangzhou had been attacked by returning Chinese laborers. When his government recalled him in 1889, he could at least claim his four years in Washington had not been entirely in vain. Unfortunately for Chang, however, the compensation package won him few plaudits. He was accused of corruption, including mishandling of the indemnification money, and his standing with the Qing rulers went from bad to worse. He was imprisoned on an accusation that he had fraudulently dealt with foreigners on a railroad concession, his property was confiscated, and he was banished to Xinjiang province. Chang's career came to a bloody end in 1900 when he was beheaded on the orders of the empress dowager, Cixi.[7]

CHAPTER TWENTY-TWO

A Second Confession

IF THE CITIZENS of Wallowa County hoped the trial would close the book on the massacre, they were sorely disappointed a few years later. On September 30, 1891, the *Walla Walla Statesman* in Walla Walla, Washington, published a confession attributed to Robert McMillan by his father, Hugh McMillan, then working as a local blacksmith. The article ran under the headline, "The Mystery Solved":

> *I make this statement from the statement made me by my son Robert, aged sixteen, just prior to his death, and by me then reduced to writing. In the latter part of April 1887, my son and Bruce Evans, J. T. Canfield, Mat Larue [sic], Frank Vaughan, Hiram Maynard, and Carl [sic] Hughes were stopping in a cattle camp four miles from Snake river. My son and Evans, Canfield, Larue, and Vaughan went to the Chinese camp on the Snake River. Canfield and Larue went above the camp and Evans and Vaughan remained below. There were thirteen Chinese in the camp and they were fired on. Twelve Chinese were instantly killed and one other caught afterwards and his brains beaten out. The party got that evening five thousand five hundred dollars in gold dust. Next day, eight more Chinese came to the camp in a boat. They were all killed and their bodies with the others thrown into the river. The party then took a boat and went to another Chinese camp four miles distance where thirteen Chinese were working on a river bar. These were all killed and their bodies thrown into the river. The camp was robbed and fifty thousand dollars in gold secured. My son was present only the first day, but was acquainted with the facts as they were talked over by the parties in his presence. The circumstances here detailed occurred on the Oregon side of the Snake river in Wallowa County near the northeast corner of the state.*
>
> *Dated Walla Walla, Aug. 3, 1891*
> *Hugh McMillan.*[1]

The newspaper added this postscript:

*The country where the massacre occurred is in the big canyon of
Snake river near the Imnaha [sic] is very inaccessible and has for the
past twenty-five years been the general rendezvous of all the horse and
cattle thieves of Oregon, Idaho and Washington. Many bodies have, at
different times, been found bearing marks of brutal treatment, in fact at
one time it was as much as a man's life was worth to hunt for his lost or
stolen stock unless accompanied by well-armed friends.*

*The Statesman takes no stock in the statement that fifty-five
thousand dollars was realized by the murders for the reason that such
rich diggings never did exist in that vicinity. Still the Chinamen must
have had considerable gold dust, as they had been working for fully six
months.*

*The statement made by Hugh McMillan only serves to clear up the
mystery, but is worthless to convict any of the murderers from a legal
standpoint.*[2]

In Wallowa County, the *Chieftain* reported the confession a month
later, on October 8, but under a San Francisco dateline, attributing the
information to Frederick Bee, China's consul, said to have given the story to
San Francisco newspapers. The *Chieftain* article begins with a background
paragraph from the unnamed San Francisco newspaper, saying the Chinese
consulate had initiated an investigation when the crime occurred "but was
then unable to find who committed the crime." After running the text of
the confession, the *Chieftain* added a paragraph it attributed to the San
Francisco newspaper. "The Chinese consul-general in this city will at once
communicate these facts to his own government, and it is probable steps
will be taken to punish the murders [sic]."[3]

The *Chieftain* followed this paragraph with its own postscript, mocking
the notion that anyone would be punished.

*To the people of Wallowa County, the revival of this old story
seems peculiar, and some of its statements absurd, especially the
announcement that steps will probably be taken to punish the murders
[sic]. The principal facts in McMillan's confession are not materially
different from those brought out at the circuit court trials, in this
county three years ago. Indictments were found against all the parties
mentioned above, and all that were tried and acquitted. Evans,*

Canfield, and Larue were never apprehended after the indictments were found, having left the county previously.[4]

The *Chieftain's* postscript didn't challenge the figure of thirty-four dead, although it had not previously reported this death toll. Probably written by the then-editor, F. M. McCully, the postscript appeared to acknowledge the accuracy of the figure by saying the "principal facts in McMillan's confession are not materially different" from those brought out at the trial. This raises the possibility that the actual number of victims was revealed during the trial. Of course, it is possible the editor simply chose not to address the specifics of McMillan's confession. Also, it was interesting to me that the postscript apparently marked the first time the *Chieftain* mentioned the trial and the outcome.

From this point on, most references to the massacre would use the higher figures of Chinese dead, some citing thirty-one victims; others, thirty-four.[5] Whichever is correct, it surpassed the twenty-eight Chinese killed at Rock Springs, Wyoming, thus making the Deep Creek massacre the worst single slaying of Chinese at the hands of whites in the American West.[6]

CHAPTER TWENTY-THREE

Blooming Flour

FIVE WEEKS BEFORE the murder trial, a newspaper in nearby Union County reported that Canfield had returned to his old haunts. It was just a paragraph in the *Oregon Scout* on July 20, 1888:

> *J. T. Canfield was seen a few days ago on the Imnaha. He is one of the Chinese murderers. He was armed with two six shooters and a Winchester rifle. He is one of the horse thieves that Nodine caught and bound over and who afterward went and shot some of the Nodine horses. It is believed that those Chinese murderers will come clear [sic], although they do not deny doing the deed.*[1]

Considering what is known about Canfield, it comes as no surprise that, after being released on bond for stealing Fred Nodine's horses, he sought revenge by killing some of the rancher's stock. But he may have had another, and more important, reason for risking capture by returning to the Imnaha Valley: he wanted the gold—not just some of the gold, apparently, but all of the gold. To get it, Horner suggested, Canfield may have double-crossed Evans by burying the gold in a place only he knew about.

Estimates of the value of gold taken by the gang from the Chinese camp ranged from the three thousand dollars mentioned in the initial *Lewiston Teller* articles, to the four thousand to five thousand dollars cited in the Slater letter, to the fifty thousand dollars in Robert McMillan's deathbed confession. As for the buried gold ingots seized by Evans and Canfield from the rancher-outlaw Douglas, Horner said he was told they were worth about seventy-five thousand dollars.[2] While McMillan's estimate of the Chinese gold was improbably high, he might have included in his estimate the value of the gold bars. But whatever the gold's precise value, it was sufficient to whet the appetite of anyone seeking a fast fortune.

No one knows whether the gang found all the Chinese gold, whether they took some of what they did find, and buried the rest, or whether they buried all of what they found. Following discovery of the massacre, miners and scavengers alike descended on Deep Creek. Horner wrote that one prospector found retorted gold in a tea can on the gravel bar, along with evidence it came from the Chinese.

> *Joseph Barnes ... while digging in a ditch to placer mine on the bar, near the mouth of this creek, found buried under a sarvus [sic] bush, a round tea can in which was $450 in retorted gold [and] a double braided human hair chain about sixteen inches long when doubled which [the can] was rusted in several places... Later he gathered up $200 more of retorted gold scattered around among the boulders.*[3]

When gold is the issue, the truth is seldom close at hand. Joseph Barnes might well have found the gold elsewhere and said it came from Deep Creek in order to throw others off the trail. Horner, however, seemed to believe this account. He said a relative of his, Charles Horner, took Barnes' newly found gold to Joseph, from where it was shipped to Boise, Idaho, and exchanged for currency. He even professed to know how Barnes spent forty dollars of the proceeds—he "bought himself a pair of good field glasses."[4]

One can only guess how the Chinese queue ended up in the tea can, or whether Barnes may have invented this detail to embellish his story.

THERE IS NO single version of what happened to the gold. Findley said the killers "cached their loot temporarily" after the killings, then designated one of their number—most likely Canfield—to dispose of it. "It was arranged that the young outlaw who planned the crime would later take the gold dust and the Douglas loot and have it minted and give each one his share when he returned."[5] If this information is correct, it contradicts Findley's earlier portrayal of Vaughan, Hughes, McMillan, and Maynard as innocent bystanders. If each was entitled to a share of the gold, it suggests they had done something to earn their share, other than stand and watch.

Horner wrote extensively about the stolen gold, which he also tried to find. He said the Chinese gold was buried, not once, but twice. Canfield and Evans, working together, buried it the first time. According to Horner's account, they also dug up the stagecoach strongbox containing the gold ingots, and reburied it separately from the Chinese gold. However, following Evans' arrest, Canfield dug up the gold from both hiding places and buried it in a new location, possibly known only to him. This suggested the double-cross of Evans. At another point in his history, Horner wrote that there might be two final hiding places. He didn't try to resolve the contradiction.

Horner reported that he had learned of the buried gold when two men from Elk City, Idaho, whom he identified as Homer Greer and William Stein, stopped at his home on Camp Creek in 1937 to ask the location of an old Nez Perce trail across Trail Creek.[6] The creek flows into Little Sheep Creek in the narrow canyon joining the Wallowa and Imnaha River valleys.

Told by Horner that the Nez Perce trail crossed Trail Creek in several places, the men asked him to accompany them and "told me what they were after." He quoted them as saying they had learned of the hiding place of the gold from a man named Link Haines, a part-Cherokee who claimed to be a distant relative of Will Rogers. Haines, they said, had learned of the hiding place directly from Canfield while working for him at a blacksmith shop in Glenns Ferry, Idaho. Canfield supposedly told Haines he had marked the hiding place with a pick and shovel, left in nearby brush. Haines was said to have found the tools, but not the gold.

Horner stated that Greer and Stein were unsuccessful in their search, but that Greer appeared later to search on his own.

> *Then he came to see me. And in September he came to see me again. He said Tite [sic] told Haines just where the cache was, as he, Bruce Evans and Omer [sic] LaRue had quite a time bringing the messenger box with the gold bars in, up from Snake River, as it contained about $75,000 and was hard to keep from slipping all the time on the pack horse. Tite said it was buried right in the old Indian trail. And when they covered it up, they drove some cattle over it, so it wouldn't show where it was buried. Tite had told his father and brother Seth where it was and they went down and searched, but claimed they could find nothing ... Greer said this was seven trips he had made to look for that cache, and believed it was there. And I told him I didn't think any one would ever find that cache.[7]*

Horner wrote this portion of his history after Stein and Greer first contacted him in 1937, so their hunt for the gold must have been fresh in his memory. He cited a specific date, September 19, 1938, when he accompanied Greer and Stein on one of their searches.[8]

Canfield's family also sought the gold. Horner reported that Canfield's sister-in-law—Seth Canfield's wife—appeared with another man to look for the gold at a place then known as Bruce Evans Basin on Pine Creek. The basin, where both Evans and Canfield had their ranches, was ten miles northwest of the supposed Trail Creek hiding place. For his sister-in-law to search that far from the Trail Creek site suggested Canfield hadn't disclosed the actual hiding place. The couple "dug around on the hillside for several days and did not find anything ... And this gold is supposed to be buried yet."[9] Canfield himself returned a year later with an unidentified woman to look for buried gold in the basin, also without success. Horner gives no date for the Canfields' search, but it was probably much earlier than when Stein and Greer appeared on the scene.

Horner's suggestion that there were two final hiding places might explain some of the confusion. It suggests the following: In the days immediately following the murders, Evans, Canfield, and LaRue buried the Chinese gold and the gold ingots in one location along Trail Creek. But following Evans' arrest, and with LaRue having fled, Canfield reburied the Chinese gold near his ranch on Pine Creek, leaving the gold bars in the first hiding place along Trail Creek. While the Chinese gold was easy to transport, the gold bars would have been difficult to move. If Horner's estimated value of seventy-five thousand dollars is correct, the ingots would have weighed nearly three hundred pounds. And because of the U.S. government stamp, they couldn't be easily sold.

Horner's speculation that the gold might still be buried in the Wallowa country was only his guess. My own guess is that when Greer and Stein knocked on Horner's door, Canfield and his sister-in-law had long since dug up the Chinese gold, leaving the gold ingots for whoever could find them. It is not unreasonable to speculate the bars remain undiscovered to this day, although not for lack of effort to find them.

CHAPTER TWENTY-FOUR

Flight

FINDLEY'S HISTORY, printed in local newspapers, includes a grainy photograph of a family gathering of eight adults and a child on a cabin front porch. The men are seated on the front step; the women are standing behind them. A caption identifies them.

> *A group of pioneer settlers taken at the Frank Vaughan cabin in the Imnaha River valley. From left to right their names are as follows. Top row Mrs. Adams, Mrs. Brumback, Mrs. Minnie Vaughan and Mrs. Betty Smith. Bottom row Newton Brumback, Frank Vaughan, Floyd Vaughan—Frank Vaughan's boy—A. N. Adams, and Joseph Smith.*[1]

Minnie is Frank's wife. The Adamses are his in-laws. The Smiths are the same aunt and uncle who had accompanied the Vaughan family on its journey from Nebraska to Oregon years earlier. Frank sits on the lower porch step, closer to the camera than the others, staring boldly ahead under heavy, furrowed brows. He's thin, even gaunt, with a four-inch goatee and a mustache. He looks to be about forty, but could be younger. Floyd, a boy of four or five, is his son. He stands behind his father's left shoulder.

No one is smiling, making it difficult to see them as a relaxed family group. Frank and Minnie's two daughters, Nellie and Ione—both older than Floyd—are not pictured. The little that the photo reveals of the Vaughan cabin shows it was built of eighteen-inch unfinished lumber, unpainted, with white caulking, typical construction for the homes of early settlers along the Imnaha River in the late nineteenth and early twentieth centuries. A curtained window is visible to the right of the porch.

The photograph may illustrate Vaughan's life following the massacre. Possibly it shows the 1908 "surprise party" for the Vaughan family, mentioned in a publication of the Hurricane Creek Grange.[2] No doubt Vaughan had quickly put the trial behind him. Little doubt, too, he'd given up the rustler life. He married Minnie Adams in 1890, raised a family, worked his ranch, and settled into community life.

In his history, Findley affectionately referred to the people in the photograph.

All of the above were good neighbors of ours. The four mothers shown
were all special friends of mothers [sic]. Mrs. Adams and Mrs. Smith
often went with her to help her care for the sick and ailing and to
help usher new babies into the world. Mrs. Smith was deeply religious
and lived up to her belief. She served as assistant Sunday school
superintendent and most of the time while father was serving as the
superintendent. Frank Vaughan and Sam Adams shown in the above
picture were my companions on many cattle roundups and grizzly
hunting trips on the Grizzly Ridge range.[3]

Vaughan appeared over the years in at least two photographs in the
Wallowa County Chieftain, suggesting he soon regained respectability in
the community—if he ever lost it. One photograph, taken in 1898, ten years
after the trial, shows him with two dozen other young men and women at
a gathering of a social group called the Joseph Bachelors' Club. Then about
age thirty, Vaughan stands unsmiling in the back row. A second undated

Frank Vaughan is in the left forefront of this photograph taken at his home in the
Imnaha River Valley in the years following the trial. Vaughan holds blacksmith
tongs in his left hand while his right arm is around a dog. His son, Floyd, is over
his left shoulder. His wife, Minnie, is second from the right in the back row. The
occasion may be a 1908 "surprise party" for the Vaughans. (Photo courtesy of the
family of Wynona Eleen Brown)

photograph shows him with his cousin, Harry, in front of the Wallowa Feed Stable.[4]

Even though Vaughan had settled into family and ranching life, he could scarcely have forgotten the massacre. He eventually would leave Wallowa County. He sold his ranch along the Imnaha River and moved to Corning in California's Tehama County with Minnie and two of their children, Ione and Floyd.[5] In the 1930 Census, when Vaughan was sixty-four, living in California, he identified himself as a farmer. He may have died soon after as he wasn't mentioned in the 1940 Census. In Horner's history, someone had written in a shaky hand in a margin that "Vaughan died in California."[6] Minnie Vaughan died in 1953 at age eighty-three.

There were those in the family who never forgave Vaughan for the massacre. A great-grandnephew, Vern Russell, told me in a 1995 interview of hearing his father's unforgiving assessment of Vaughan's role. "Father told me old Frank was guilty as sin," said Russell, then seventy-five. Russell was the retired public works director for Wallowa County and raised ostriches on his farm outside of Joseph. Over coffee at a Joseph restaurant, he tried to be helpful, remembering conversation around the dinner table about "the family's skeleton in the closet." But he recalled no detail of Vaughan's involvement. "I can't remember my mother ever discussing it ... It doesn't bother me any, but apparently it wasn't too well received by the rest of the Vaughan family."[7] Russell died in 2002 at age eighty-two.

THERE ARE GOOD reasons to reread one's research, not just once, but several times. At least this applies to me. Overlooked in my initial reading of Findley's history was his appreciation on the last page to those who "assisted me." Among them are "my schoolmates in the first school in the Imnaha River Valley ... who gave me valuable assistance and encouragement." And among these, he singles out several by name, including Frank Vaughan.[8] I'm going to guess it was Vaughan who provided Findley with much of the detail about the schoolyard plot to kill the Chinese and the massacre that followed. In so doing, Vaughan may have shaped an interpretation of events that downplayed his participation to make it appear he was little more than a bystander.

WHEN BRUCE "BLUE" Evans fled Wallowa County, he left behind his wife, Josephine, and his children, Walter, age five, and Veronica, age three. There is no indication in any of the settlers' journals, or in other accounts, that he ever returned to the county. However, if he had returned, there is no reason to believe anyone would have turned him in. Josephine divorced Evans two years after the trial and was awarded his property in the uncontested divorce. She later remarried and continued to reside in Wallowa County.

Horner reported Evans was seen in Wyoming in 1920, using the name Billie McGuire.[9] There was another report that Evans left the country. Sister Alfreda Elsensohn, the late writer-historian at Monastery of St. Gertrude in Cottonwood, Idaho, wrote that the leader of the gang—she didn't mention his name, but it was probably Evans—may have fled to South America. She attributed this information to a Captain E. G. MacFarlane, manager of a Snake River transportation company.[10] No one else suggested Evans or any other of the killers left the country, but that doesn't mean it didn't happen.

MORE IS KNOWN about Titus Canfield. Horner reported that he later served up to ten years in the Kansas Penitentiary for stealing some mules. Following his release, he returned to Oregon to search for the buried gold, then moved to Texas, where he married and raised a family. Horner didn't say where in Texas, and he may not have known, as he reported none of these events with any certainty. From Texas, he believed that Canfield next moved to Idaho where, under the name of Charley Canfield, he operated a blacksmith shop at Glenns Ferry, seventy miles east of Boise and three hundred miles from Enterprise.[11]

A Charles Canfield is buried with his wife, Jennie, under what Donna Carnahan of Glenns Ferry described as the largest headstone in Glenns Rest Cemetery. Mrs. Carnahan, whose grandmother's sister married into the Canfield family, told me she hadn't known that this was the same Canfield involved in the Chinese massacre. However, her research on my behalf helped confirm it beyond doubt. In the same cemetery plot are the graves of Hiram and Mary E. Canfield, "Father" and "Mother" inscribed on their headstones. These are the names of Canfield's parents. Buried in the same plot are a Hezekiah and Minnie Bayles—this is probably Canfield's sister, who brought provisions to his hideout following the massacre. In

Burial site in Glenns Ferry, Idaho, of Titus Canfield, one of accused killers of the Chinese gold miners. Canfield, who escaped from Oregon, later settled in Idaho after changing his first name to Charles. He ran a livery stable, possibly financed by gold taken from the Chinese miners. He died in 1929. (Photo by Duston Fink)

the 1910 Census, Charles Canfield, then forty-six, listed his occupation as "blacksmith shop." Also, the year listed for his birth, 1866, and birthplace, Indiana, are those of Titus Canfield.[12]

Canfield's wife was the former Jennie B. Powell. They were married in Texas in 1892. Canfield died in 1929 at age sixty-three. Jennie, twelve years younger, died in 1963. They had one child, Roy, born in 1895 in what is now Burkburnett, Texas. Roy identified himself in the 1920 Census as owner of a blacksmith shop in Gooding, Idaho, thirty-two miles east of Glenns Ferry. He died in Boise in 1947 at about age fifty-two, and is buried near his parents.

I found it revealing that the newspaper obituaries for Mary and Hiram Canfield made no mention of their years in the Wallowa country. They were sent to me by a Canfield descendant, Kimberly England of Saratoga, California: Mary died in 1914, Hiram in 1917. Hiram's obituary said the family moved from Iowa to Oregon's Grande Ronde Valley in 1876, and then to a ranch at Kings Hill Creek near Glenns Ferry about 1887. Mary's obituary in the Glenns Ferry newspaper was more specific, saying they moved to Kings Hill Creek in the fall of 1887, which would have been just months after their son jumped bail on the rustling charge and fled Wallowa County. Even though Mary Canfield would later forfeit her son's bail, the proximity of Canfield to his parents suggested they were on good terms. Gold may have kept the family together.

My conversation with Donna Carnahan led me to Janet Jeffries of Boise, a granddaughter of Roy Canfield, and to Kimberly England, Jeffries' aunt. Jeffries said she had never heard her great-grandfather's name mentioned, although as a young girl she remembered meeting her great-grandmother,

Jennie. Looking back, she said the anonymity of her great-grandfather struck her as odd.[13] England sent me valuable geneaological information on the Canfield family.

The bizarre interweaving of the families with connections to the events surrounding the massacre continued into the next generation. Roy Canfield married Maude Branscom, the daughter of George D. Branscom, who almost certainly is the same George D. Branscom who testified before the Circuit Court grand jury that, in 1888, indicted Canfield and the others for the Chinese massacre.

DID CANFIELD RETRIEVE some or all of the gold buried in Wallowa County, and use it to start a new life? The evidence suggests he did. As noted above, Horner wrote that Canfield returned to Oregon to look for the gold following his release from prison. He then took up a new life in Texas and Idaho—with enough money to own a blacksmith shop.

What I find inexplicable is why no effort was made to arrest Canfield, to hold him accountable for the murder and rustling charges still hanging over his head. His family had kept his secret—his wife and son may not have known it, although his parents and siblings surely did. However, as Horner apparently knew a great deal about Canfield's whereabouts, and his search for the stolen gold, others must have known too. But perhaps Canfield didn't need to keep his past a secret. By the turn of the century, the massacre may have been largely forgotten in Wallowa County, and those who did remember didn't care that one of the killers lived prosperously in the next state.

OF OTHER GANG members, there is scant information. McMillan's family soon moved from the county and the boy was dead within a year, presumably of natural causes, possibly a victim of diptheria.[14] Horner said Hughes also was dead by the time he was writing, but didn't say when he died, or give the circumstances. Of Maynard, there's no further mention, or record, although Wallowa County marriage licenses show a William Maynard, most likely a relation, married a woman named Elizabeth on September 21, 1888, with John Hughes, Hezekiah's brother, as a witness.

LaRue, like Evans, dropped from sight. David Stratton wrote of rumors circulating in the county years later that LaRue was killed in a poker game somewhere in California.[15]

A seventh member of the gang, Andy Beckelheimer, wasn't implicated in the massacre. But apparently, he later did go to prison. A handwritten notation in Horner's journal says, "Beckelheimer got caught last and was sent to the pen for two years for stealing a span of trask horses from W. K. Stubblefield."[16] The reference to a trask horse may indicate the horses came from the Trask Ranch in Wyoming, known for producing prize quarterhorses.

There's nothing to indicate Evans, Canfield, and LaRue ever saw one another again after fleeing the county. However, it's not out of the question that they rendezvoused months, or even years later, to divide up the loot. What is certain is that once they fled the county, authorities made no effort to track them down, and offered no explanation that survives for failing to do so.

JUDGE VINCENT APPARENTLY played no further role in the case following the arrest and indictments of the gang members in 1888. He moved that same year from Lewiston to Cottonwood, eighty miles southeast of Lewiston, and moved again in 1891 to nearby Mt. Idaho, where he operated a hotel for six years. He won election to a two-year term as probate judge, but was defeated for re-election. Vincent was still U.S. commissioner as late as 1892 when records show he presided over a hearing in Mt. Idaho on a counterfeiting case.

Vincent's Mt. Idaho hotel is long gone, as are the other buildings in what once was a prosperous community. The town is reached today on a winding rural road. When I last visited, the town consisted of a smattering of modest homes, a Methodist church, and a few abandoned structures tangled in blackberry vines.[17] The town's past glory is spelled out for passersby on a roadside marker, which identifies it as the one-time county seat, a status lost to nearby Grangeville after Mt. Idaho refused to allow a grange within town limits. The marker also says Mt. Idaho once had "an important Chinese community."

Vincent died in Mt. Idaho on March 21, 1909 at age eighty-six. If he felt his investigation into the Hells Canyon massacre was a significant event in his life, he apparently kept it to himself, as it is not mentioned in his obituaries or in other accounts of his life.

THERE HAVE BEEN occasional inquiries about the massacre over the years. An Oregon congressman, Walter Pierce, asked Secretary of State Cordell Hull about the case in 1936, receiving from Hull a reply on March 24, 1936, that the 1888 compensation paid to the Chinese on January 11, 1889 "of course included among a number of other cases the Chinese murdered in 1887 in Oregon."[18] Hull may have assumed the matter was resolved. But his predecessors had ignored the fact that the massacre had not been among the claims submitted by the Chinese government, and, in any event, the Chinese had mentioned only ten victims, not the final toll of as many as thirty-four. Indeed, the Chinese had specifically excluded the Hells Canyon murders because so little was known about them. For the Chinese, there has never been a resolution of the massacre.

Pierce had his own bias against Chinese. A Democrat, Pierce was elected governor of Oregon in 1922 with support from the Ku Klux Klan. While governor, he supported Oregon's 1923 Alien Land Law prohibiting Chinese and Japanese from owning land in the state. After one term, he was defeated for re-election, but later served five terms in Congress.[19]

THE NATION'S EXCLUSION laws remained in force against Chinese laborers until World War II when President Franklin D. Roosevelt persuaded Congress to repeal them on December 17, 1943.

PART THREE

P. S. Keeping Secrets

CHAPTER TWENTY-FIVE

The Secret Keepers

Snow, crusted and grey with age, covers the sidewalk and steps leading to the front door of Marjorie Martin's pleasant white bungalow in Enterprise. Since the front steps aren't shoveled, I presume Martin uses the screened side porch, where the snow is cleared. But I hesitate to bang on the porch door. For my meeting with Martin, I want to do things right. I want to know what she knows, and I don't want to give her any reason not to help me. Frankly, I'm also a little nervous.

I had been told by several people that Martin might be the key to the lost and misplaced records, including those found in the county safe. "There is no way you can convince me that someone in that courthouse as long as Marjorie Martin was, did not have a pretty good idea what was in that safe," said Bruce Womack, the retired Forest Service archeologist.[1] Martin, eighty-seven at the time of this visit, worked in the courthouse for forty-seven years, the last forty-five as county clerk. She retired in 1987.

I crunch up Martin's front steps, careful not to slip on the packed snow, wet from the unseasonably warm March sunshine. The tired snowdrifts piled along the streets and across shaded front lawns may be the last of it for this year.

The buzzer works.

Marjorie Martin, one of the "secret keepers." The long-time Wallowa County clerk acknowledged hiding records of the massacre and trial. She said it was for safekeeping. (Photo by the author)

I have been here before, when Martin would scarcely talk to me. But she told me on the phone the other day she now has something to say, so I've driven up from Portland, yet another trip to the Wallowa Valley in pursuit of the massacre story.

Martin's home is on Grant Street, a quiet street two blocks from the courthouse. The house, a bungalow of post-World War II vintage, appears in good shape except for a sagging gutter over the porch door. The broken gutter could necessitate some fancy footwork for anyone using that entrance in a rainstorm. But rain is infrequent here during the spring and summer. Residents of eastern Oregon laugh at the state's national reputation as rain soaked. Indeed, the two-thirds of the state lying east of the Cascades is mostly high desert, with far more sagebrush than green grass.

It has always required a hardy bunch to live in the Wallowa country, enduring its cold winters and dry summers, semi-isolated within the region's moat-like gorges and granite peaks. As with many other rural communities, the county's resource-based economy was in free-fall. Two of three lumber mills were shut down, and the future of the third was by no means assured. After the Idaho Northern & Pacific Railroad halted its daily trains into the Wallowa Valley in 1997, the county bought the railroad in a long-shot bid to return it to profitability by running excursions for tourists. During the five years when the railroad was idle, with weeds growing from the tracks that snake across the valley, school buses continued to dutifully stop at the railroad crossings. For the most part, the Wallowa country is a law-abiding place. Did I say, for the most part?

Something to think about as I press the buzzer a second time.

During my drives to Wallowa County, sometimes for just a day or two, others for a week or more, I have been drawn to the endless beauty of its rivers and mountains, and the enduring fabric of a community where many of the inhabitants descend from the first settlers, people such as the Boswells, the Womacks, and the Findleys. On my visits, I avoid making unnecessary mention that I am a reporter, as out-of-town reporters are on the same list of undesirables for many residents as environmentalists. Until a recent influx of Latino farm workers, there were almost no minorities among the county's 7,226 residents in the 2000 Census. The number of Nez Perce residents could be counted on one hand, with fingers to spare. This is not unlike the racial makeup in other rural communities in the West—whites pass mostly whites on streets and sidewalks; sports pages, with rare exceptions, reveal exclusively white players on the high school basketball and football teams, and mostly white faces smile out from school yearbooks. Wallowa County must have been one of the few in the nation without a Chinese restaurant until the Mi Ling restaurant opened in Enterprise in 2003.

Once, before the restaurant opened, I asked Martin whether she wished the valley had a Chinese restaurant. She replied it didn't matter to her. She bought her Chinese food at the Safeway.

More to think about as I listen for footsteps.

With Marjorie Martin it is important to be on time, I assume. But even as I push the buzzer for the third time, I know she will not be. I retreat to my room at the Ponderosa Motel across from the courthouse to wait.

I DIDN'T KNOW what Martin wanted to tell me, but I hoped to learn from her an answer to the question that continued to bedevil me: why would a gang of outwardly respectable ranchers and schoolboys plot the slaughter of nearly three dozen defenseless Chinese when they easily could have robbed them without the bloodshed? Frank Vaughan's explanation that the Chinese were killed because they refused to loan the gang a boat was laughable. And I had this corollary question: why did the people of Wallowa County care so little about the crime that they would honor the leader of the gang of killers on a memorial arch for early settlers, and do nothing to acknowledge his victims?

I might find answers in the trial journal. But where was the journal? I never lost hope it might still exist because whoever had hidden the documents in the safe might also have secreted away the journal. It was probably someone with access to official records who might hide them, but, out of professional ethics, never destroy them. Someone like Marjorie Martin.

I had gone to see Martin the first time at Charlotte McIver's suggestion—McIver succeeded Martin as the elected county clerk. Martin's work in the county clerk's office covered nearly half of the county's history. Possibly, just possibly, McIver said Martin might know the whereabouts—or fate—of a trial journal, if there ever was one.

On that first visit, Martin received me politely, but her anxious movements and quick short answers to my questions suggested an eagerness to see me gone. She insisted she had never seen the records in the safe, nor had any idea how they got there—"I absolutely never did see those." She also had no idea as to the whereabouts of the trial journal, and insisted she knew nothing of importance about the massacre.

"I think people have a right to know there was a Chinese massacre, but I think it's just as well to go on and forget it," she told me.[2] "It's a sad story." Getting nowhere, I was about to leave when she called to me at the door. "There were more than ten Chinese killed; I'm sure of that." At the time, that was important information for me, since I was still trying to reconcile the wide disparity between the official reports of ten victims and the later reports of as many as thirty-four killed.

I wasn't through with Martin, but she was, on that visit, through with me.

I HAD NEXT turned to Grace Bartlett, a county historian who later became a dear friend until her death. Grace—I would come to know her by her first name—also didn't want to talk about the massacre, and sought to discourage me from writing a news story. She knew of the murders, of course, but insisted they were committed by outsiders, not "the good, hard-working people" who had settled the valley.

"I have no interest in that story,'" said Grace, then eighty-three. "People in the early days came to make homes. These are the kind of people I'm talking about, the ones who came and settled, a fine bunch of people." She

Grace Bartlett, another of the "secret keepers." The Wallowa County historian at first objected to the author's efforts to uncover details of the massacre at Deep Creek, but later provided valuable help. (Photo by Elane Dickenson, Wallowa County Chieftain)

said the killers, the rustlers, had nothing to do with these "fine bunch of people," and dismissed outright any evidence to the contrary.[3]

In a letter to the editor of the *Chieftain*, Grace had already denounced the newspaper's account of the records found in the courthouse safe, and the suggestion they had been hidden as part of a cover-up.

> [I]n regard to the records found in the county clerk's office plus the conjectures and insinuations aired in that Chieftain, I would like to point out that the old adage, 'The truth will set you free' is a good and useful one, but that I doubt if the truth was well served in your paper that day.[4]

When my story based on the documents appeared in *The Oregonian*, Grace was distressed by what she felt was unfavorable publicity for the county and a blot on the good name of its settlers. But she never said with what, specifically, she found fault. Her objection was straightforward: she didn't think the story should be resurrected, notwithstanding that it had never been fully aired in the *Chieftain*, or anywhere else. For Grace, the massacre wasn't part of the county's history at all, at least not the history she wanted people to know.

Nonetheless, Grace and I became friends, occasionally drinking beer together while perusing early county maps and other documents spread out on the large braided rug on her living-room floor. Her home was surprisingly humble. But it had a friendly feel to it, and I enjoyed those visits. The house was flat roofed, with a stovepipe chimney, unpainted rough-hewn board walls inside, and exterior walls covered in a green composition material. Grace had built the home on a forty-acre ranch west of Joseph with her second husband, Harry Bartlett, a Nez Perce. The couple bred thoroughbreds, which they raced throughout the West.

During the years I knew her, Grace lived alone, surrounded by books that spilled from the crammed shelves throughout her home. While she had electric heating, Grace preferred the warmth of a wood stove, which also kept warm her coffee pot. She parked her aging yellow Jeep Wagoneer in her occasionally overgrown front yard—there was no front walk or driveway. For years after her death, I would drive by and see the car still parked there.

Grace was polite to a fault, seldom smiled, and laughed even less. She had a patrician bearing that would seem to make her more at home in New England than in the rough-and-tumble Wallowa Valley. Although illness drained her energy in her final years, and her frequent notes to me were written in an evermore shaky hand, I never heard her complain.

Among Grace's hundreds of books were several county histories she had written, none of which mentioned the massacre. But one did offer a clue to the cover-up. In her 1992 book, *From the Wallowas*, Grace included a chapter on the historian Horner, with whom she had worked and obviously much admired. She wrote of Horner, who died in 1969 at age eighty-three, that he had taken to heart advice from another prominent Oregon historian, George Simes, to avoid embarrassing anyone when writing history. Grace wrote that Simes' admonition to Horner was: "Put everything down, except things that will hurt individuals." She went on:

> *In keeping with this injunction, which became a religion with him, Mr. Horner has said now and then in his manuscript, 'a certain man' or has left a blank space for a man's name. This may irritate the future gossip mongers who will someday comb his manuscript for startling stories on how the old pioneers lived, but it will leave no great gap. Mr. Simes knew he was advising one who had been a friend, neighbor, and acquaintance of most of the people or their close relations who had been makers of early Wallowa County history and he counseled him well.*[5]

Thus, I found myself categorized among the "gossip mongers," as Grace, in her own writing, left no doubt her views paralleled those of Horner in her respect for the early settlers and her resolve to protect their reputations.

> *Looking backward at these early settlers, as we are able to do now, it's easy not to be surprised at the high quality of this small group of people. We now know what they and their children and their children's children have done. We have seen the trees they planted, the houses they built. Actually it shouldn't have been too hard for anyone to have guessed this from the beginning. Pictures ... show us a fine-looking lot of hard-working and resolute people.*[6]

A few more words about Grace. She had made the Wallowa Valley her home since 1932, the year she married a local resident, Alfred Butterfield. They had two children before the marriage ended in divorce. Her father was Robert W. Sawyer, a Harvard Law School graduate who had moved to Oregon from the East Coast and became publisher of the *Bend Bulletin* in central Oregon.[7] Once Grace moved to the Wallowa Valley, I doubt she ever looked back. She wrote in her book *Wallowa Country* that "this country gives herself to and enriches the minds (if not always the pockets) of those who love her" (the parenthetical insert is hers).[8] The valley became her refuge, and fueled her considerable energies. In return, she gave back her unqualified loyalty.

In her later years, Grace was something of a recluse. She drove daily to her work as volunteer curator at the Wallowa County Museum, which she had helped establish in an old bank building on Joseph's Main Street. She would arrive at the museum in the early morning hours, leaving before it opened for the day. Grace died in 1999 at age eighty-seven. I regret I only knew her in her later years.

MARJORIE MARTIN FINALLY answers her telephone. She asks me over, apologizes for being late, explains she was getting her hair done. She admits me through the screened porch, under the loose gutter. It is not raining today.

Martin's living room is simply furnished, with beige wall-to-wall carpeting. The room is dominated by two large stuffed chairs, one pink and the other dark green, placed at right angles to a curtainless picture window looking into a large backyard where patches of soggy brown grass are winning a competition with the slushy snow. On the wall next to the window is a framed picture of a laughing red-cheeked Santa Claus, a faux Norman Rockwell painting. A grand piano and another chair are along the opposite wall. The only disorder in the room is a coffee table piled high with papers and magazines. There is no invitation to see the rest of the house.

Martin chooses the pink chair, which blends nicely with her lighter pink cardigan sweater. She doesn't invite me to sit down, and, after standing awkwardly for a minute or so, I seat myself in the chair next to the piano, facing the window. Martin is to my left. Her hair, white with just a touch of gray, is freshly coiffed. *For my visit?* Never married, Martin shares her home with a woman of her own age whom she didn't introduce on my first visit, and doesn't again now. The other woman takes the green stuffed chair to Martin's left, closest to the picture window. I later learn she is Alice Lessman, and she and Martin have lived together for most of their adult lives.

As they sit side by side in their stuffed chairs, Martin defers frequently to Lessman for help on dates and events in her life. Each has her frailties. Martin answers my questions slowly and haltingly, occasionally stumbling over words and syntax; Lessman has difficulty walking. But together, they remember a great deal when they choose to. A shy almost demure smile never leaves Martin's face. She is polite but radiates an aura of privacy, befitting a woman who I am told knows all of the community's secrets worth knowing, and then some.

Martin explains she could not talk on my previous visit because her good friend down the street, Helen Falconer, was then still alive and she had not wanted to say anything to embarrass her. And who was Helen Falconer that she would somehow compel Martin's silence? Well, Martin discloses, Falconer was the granddaughter of Bruce Evans, leader of the gang of rustlers and killers.

I can't say I'm shocked to learn this, but Martin definitely has my attention.

Falconer's mother was Veronica Evans, one of the two children abandoned by Evans when he fled Wallowa County after his escape from the privy. With Falconer now gone, Martin says she feels free to talk. A later check will reveal that her friend died in 1994, a year before our first interview. But never mind. This is a significant revelation that opens up other potential avenues of inquiry, although Martin tries to shut them off.

I ask her why Helen Falconer didn't want the story told. She replies it wasn't Falconer's decision.

"I didn't want the story told. She was the nicest friend I had. She didn't care."

Martin says Falconer didn't have any relatives she knew of—"I think they all passed away"—which turns out not to be true. And she says they never discussed Bruce Evans. It is hard to believe this is true either, especially from someone who had, by all accounts, made it her business to know everything about everyone in the county. But knowing isn't telling. She does not think Evans ever contacted his family after fleeing the county.

As the conversation wanders, Martin says she was thrust into the job of county clerk in 1941 when her predecessor and mentor, D. B. Reavis, abruptly left the county to take a job elsewhere.

This strikes me as another significant revelation: The signature of county clerk D. B. Reavis appears on many of the trial documents from the courthouse safe. I haven't yet done the math in my head, but I imagine Reavis must have been in his teens when he was first elected county clerk. Did he hide the documents?

"I knew Mr. Reavis," says Martin. "He was a nice man. He liked to play poker."

Martin has difficulty explaining, so she goes into another room and returns with a printed list of all the county clerks of Wallowa County. The name D. B. Reavis appears twice, the father and the son. I shouldn't be surprised. This is yet another example of descendants of the original settlers occupying parallel positions of importance.

The conversation drags on for nearly a half-hour, with Martin not offering much else, and I am beginning to think she has told me all she intends to tell. But just when I'm about to leave, Martin rises and crosses the room to the coffee table, fumbling through the jumbled papers for something she at first can't find, then finds. It's a typewritten copy of the missing article on the massacre, the one that appeared in the *Wallowa County Chieftain* on April 19, 1888, the one for which, months earlier, I had spent fruitless hours searching. Martin indicates, without quite saying, that she copied the article herself. She doesn't know where the original is.

That's it for a while. Then after more small talk about her life, she recalls she once met the mother of the fifteen-year-old gang member, Robert McMillan, when the mother visited the offices of the now-defunct newspaper, the *Chief Joseph Herald,* where Martin worked as a linotype operator in the early 1930s.

Martin says the mother wanted to talk about the crime and the trial. "She told me enough to be pretty good. Yes, she did. We were interested, all of us. We were very nice to her." Martin later visited the mother at her home in Boise and learned more, but doesn't, or won't, recall specifics from either conversation.

As the afternoon progresses, Martin is on her feet more frequently, looking through the papers on the coffee table, finding more documents, some useful, some not. Among them is her own twenty-five-page fictionalized account of the massacre, which she says she wrote with another woman "just for fun."

And yes, she finally acknowledges, she is the one who locked the trial records in the safe decades earlier.

"I didn't want to lose it," is her only explanation. By "it," she means an envelope containing the records. She found it "down in a bag," she says. "It took me a long time to find it, and I worked there. They never, after I got it, asked for it. They didn't find it the first time." I'm not able to determine whom she means by "they." Reporters, perhaps?

Sometimes it is easy to understand Martin; sometimes it's not, making me wonder whether she has had a small stroke, or whether she is purposely garbling answers to questions she would rather not answer. She is especially unintelligible when I ask if she thinks there was a cover-up. She answers in the affirmative, but then I am not sure she means to say that at all. When I ask if she thinks McMillan and the others who were on trial were guilty, I cannot, even after several tries, understand her answer.

But when the subject is the Chinese, she has an easier time making herself understood. She says the settlers "didn't like them." When I ask her why, she says she doesn't know. "I often wondered about that, too." But then she adds, "Of course they were going to get all the gold, and the rest of them didn't like that." By them, she apparently means either the people in the county, or the gang of killers, I'm not sure which.

Martin seems not to understand when I ask why she thinks the gang killed the Chinese, rather than just taking their gold. "They wanted the money," she says. When I persist, she adds, "I just think that at time, you liked yourself pretty well, but you didn't want anybody else. The gun was to take care of everybody. It's always been that way. People come and don't want others to come." If I understand her correctly, she is saying the Chinese were unwelcome to the point that the Evans gang felt justified in killing them. Martin goes on to draw an improbable parallel to current attitudes toward newcomers from California, saying many people in the county want them to stay away, although she welcomes them.

About the missing trial record, she at first says she might find it for me at the courthouse, offering to return sometime to look for it, but not now. But then she questions whether there ever was such a document, suggesting that maintaining a detailed trial record might have been beyond the capabilities of the court in the county's early days, when records were written in longhand.

I've been here two hours. Martin is tiring. When I rise to leave, she apologizes for not being able to remember more. But her parting comment is perhaps as telling as anything she has told me so far.

"There is so little to know, and I think what was known was forgotten."

Intentionally or not, Martin has a way of tossing me a gem of a quote when our meetings end.

THE TRAIL GROWS faint, but it hasn't yet ended. I want to know more about Helen Falconer, and try to locate her obituary in the *Chieftain*. Surely there was one. I'm stymied at first because it turns out I don't have the correct name. Martin made her friend's name sound like "Helene Faulkner" and has indicated an incorrect year for her death. But with the help of the Bollman Funeral Home, the only funeral home in Enterprise, I learn her correct name and the year of her death, 1994.

Helen Falconer was eighty-nine when she died. Her obituary does indeed list her mother as Veronica Evans Riley, one of Bruce Evans' children by his wife, Josephine. And, although Marjorie claimed that Falconer had no surviving relatives, her obituary lists two cousins. One is Pauline Knowles of Walla Walla, Washington. Knowles, when I reach her by telephone, seems pleased to tell me the little that she knows.

She says her cousin knew her grandfather as "kind of a hard man who probably had a temper."[9] She says rather matter-of-factly that Evans returned on occasion to Wallowa County, bringing presents, which, if true, would be a revelation of considerable importance. But, when I press for details, she said she may have Evans mixed up with a relative of Levi Riley, whom Josephine married in 1890 after divorcing Evans. I silently berate myself for being too eager in my follow-up.

Josephine Evans' connections to the gang of killers went beyond her husband; she was the daughter of Thomas and Sarah Hughes and sister of gang member Hezekiah Hughes. The Evans' daughter, Veronica Evans

Riley, married Ross Falconer in 1904. Their daughter, Helen Falconer, Martin's friend, never married. She taught school in California, returning to Enterprise in 1964.

Pauline Knowles says Falconer knew her grandfather was the same Bruce Evans who led the gang of killers. She had discussed it with Knowles, who has no reluctance in addressing the silence around the massacre.

"I knew it was a scandal the family wanted to keep quiet, but it got out," she says. "They were embarrassed, of course, and just as soon preferred people in Enterprise didn't know about it. But now everybody is dead, so it doesn't matter."

She also reveals that Martin is a cousin of hers on her father's side, which creates a distant family link between Martin and Evans. Knowles says that by coincidence she plans to travel to Enterprise in the next week or so to visit Martin, and volunteers to ask about the massacre. But when I call back after that visit, she reports she was not able to learn anything beyond what she has already told me. She also discourages me from coming to Walla Walla to talk directly with her, saying she probably won't be home. Maybe I'm just being paranoid, but I wonder whether Martin asked her not to talk further with me.

I doubt I can ever prove it, but I do think it likely Evans returned to the county to see his children—and possibly retrieve some of the gold—and no one gave him away. Indeed, from what I have learned about the county's history, and its proclivity to rally around its own, I think Evans could have walked down Main Street, holding a sign with his name and the crimes he was accused of, and no one would have cared.

THAT SUMMER, I am at Martin's door again, this time with my wife, Candise. We are passing through, I explain, and want to say hello. Martin graciously admits us, although it soon becomes apparent that we have interrupted an argument. Alice Lessman seems displeased to see us. While we talk in front of the picture window, Lessman noisily rattles pots and pans in the kitchen. After ten minutes or so, she emerges from the kitchen with a walker and shuffles past us toward the patio door leading to the backyard.

"I'm going to change the sprinklers," she announces.

Martin doesn't even look at her. "You'll get wet," she says.

While Martin pays Lessman no attention at all, Candise and I watch transfixed as Lessman goes into the yard, and, supporting herself on her walker, kicks and drags the sprinkler about ten feet, an impressive and unique feat deserving of our silent applause.

There is nothing more to learn from Martin. Not surprisingly, she hasn't returned to the courthouse to look for any more papers, and I don't press her to do so now. Charlotte McIver has told me she is confident nothing relating to the trial is still to be found in her office. She has been through it all.

CHAPTER TWENTY-SIX

And Now, the Journal

THE TRIAL JOURNAL was never far from my mind. But I would have to be lucky to find it.

I was lucky.

I had taken my son, Jeffrey, to a doctor's appointment in Salem, the state capital, forty miles south of Portland. As the appointment would take several hours, leaving me time to kill, I decided to visit the nearby building housing the state archives. I wanted to see what, if anything, was in their files from Wallowa County.

It was almost too easy. A researcher handed me a loose-leaf notebook listing historic files, and their locations, in Oregon's thirty-six counties. On the first two pages of the section for Wallowa County, I ran my finger over lists of patent records, foreclosures, marriage licenses, mining claims, the county court docket, federal land grants, and a register of prisoners—all said to be properly filed in the Wallowa County clerk's vault, none of them helpful. When I turned to the third page, it took me a few moments to realize what I was seeing. There, half-way down the page, was this listing: "Circuit Court Journal, Volume A, 1887-1893." Location: the county planning department records vault. No rhyme. No reason. The planning department vault, one place I had never looked and one of the last places I would expect to find it.

As soon as I could arrange it, I returned again to Enterprise. I called ahead to see if anyone at the planning department knew of the journal. I was referred to the county clerk's office. And so, one afternoon, I dropped in unannounced at the planning department, located in the unfinished basement of the courthouse—a reflection, I guessed, of the low status in which planning is held in conservative Wallowa County. Upon learning the reason for my visit, the affable planning director, Bill Oliver, told me such a journal would likely be in the county clerk's vault. When I told him of the listing in the state archives, he recalled a recent visit by a state researcher and invited me to look for myself. Then he joined me.

The Wallowa County Courthouse was built with walk-in vaults on each floor. As far as I know, none is ever locked. At one end of the five-by-ten foot planning vault, Oliver removed a stack of boxed office supplies from in front of a bookshelf filled with dusty volumes, and began rummaging around a lower shelf, while I searched the vault from the other end. When Oliver called out, "Here it is," I felt as if a beam of heavenly light had descended on me. Oliver pointed toward a shelf still partially blocked by nondescript boxes. Leaning over his shoulder, I at first saw only a dozen or so stacked volumes of tax assessor records, bound with green covers. But farther down, one book caught my eye, the volume at the bottom of the pile, bound in a gray cover, "Circuit Court Journal, Volume A, 1887-1893."

I WISH I could say the journal contained major revelations about the trial. It did not. What it did do, however, was to raise another mystery.

The journal entries were handwritten in ink on eleven-by-nine-inch pages of heavy paper, all well preserved and easy to read. As I suspected, the presiding judge at the trial was Judge Isom, who signed the journal entries. The trial opened with jury selection on August 29, 1888, a day earlier than the documents in the safe indicated, but adjourned to the next day because of an insufficient number of names in the jury pool. This led me to wonder whether some of the names listed on subpoenas as defense witnesses were actually potential jurors. The trial resumed on August 30 with a new jury pool, from which a twelve-person jury, all men, was selected.

The entry for August 30 was dismayingly brief. Following the jury selection, Isom wrote:

> [T]he cause proceeded to trial and the jurors proceeded to hear the opening remarks of counsel and the testimony of witnesses whereupon the court ordered the further hearing of this cause to be continued until 9:30 o'clock August 31st, 1888.[1]

However, on turning the page, I found no entry for August 31, a Friday, the day the trial was to resume. A blank page looked up at me. There was no explanation. The next entry was for September 1, where Judge Isom wrote "the same jurors as of yesterday proceeded to hear further testimony for the state and for the defendants," after which the jury left the courtroom to deliberate. This was followed by the jury's verdict. I turned back to the blank page. Significantly, I found no other blank pages in the journal. If the trial had been delayed because of an illness, or for other good cause, there would have been no reason to leave an open page. I began to suspect that August 31 was the most revealing day of the trial, since the previous day had been occupied in large part by jury selection and opening statements. Did the blank page reflect a decision by Judge Isom, or the unidentified court clerk, to omit information that might prove embarrassing, or incriminating, to the defendants and their families? Might the page have been left open so the judge, or clerk, might enter the information at a later date to complete the record? I suspect the answer to both of these questions is yes, but there is no way I can ever know for certain.

This was the verdict, virtually unchanged from the version in the safe:

In the Circuit Court for State of Oregon County of Wallowa, the State of Oregon versus Hiram Maynard, Robert McMillan and Hezekiah Hughes indicted under the name of Carl Hughes, implicated with T. J. [sic] Canfield, Bruce Evans and C. O. Larue [sic], defendants.

We the jury in the above-entitled action find the said defendants Hiram Maynard, Robert McMillan, and Hezekiah Hughes not guilty.

William Green

Foreman.[2]

Following the verdict, Judge Isom released the defendants and ordered bail returned to those who had posted it. He also returned the one thousand dollar bond for Frank Vaughan. A separate order continued the murder charges against Evans, Canfield, and LaRue.

Included in the journal was Isom's May 15, 1887, order—issued during his vacation in Baker City—setting bond for Maynard, McMillan, and Hughes in response to the petition filed by the thirty-four county residents.

Another interesting tidbit in the journal was Judge Isom's dismissal of Frank Vaughan's father, Enoch Vaughan, as a grand juror from a case in March 22, 1888. While the judge said the elder Vaughan was dismissed because of "sickness in his family,"[3] another explanation seemed more likely. March 22 probably was the day Frank testified before the grand jury, which returned its murder indictments against the other members of the Evans gang the following day, on March 23.

Also recorded were the proceedings in the rustling case against Evans and Canfield. When Canfield failed to appear for arraignment on August 25,

1887, the judge ordered forfeiture of the eight hundred dollars posted by Evans and Mary Canfield, now buried beside her son in Idaho. The judge's order noted that Evans and Mary Canfield also failed to respond to an order to appear in court. Mary Canfield later paid the forfeited bail on behalf of both Evans and herself. Subsequent entries continued the rustling charges against both Canfield and Evans—two continuations for each outlaw.

OBVIOUSLY, I DID not learn from the journal what I had hoped to learn. There was no detail of the opening or closing arguments of the attorneys, or of testimony by prosecution and defense witnesses. In that sense it was disappointing. However, I at least gained the satisfaction of knowing I had tracked down the last major missing piece of documentary evidence, and learned just about everything it was still possible to learn about the massacre, one hundred and twenty years later.

After I had finished reading the journal, and copied the relevant pages on a planning department copy machine—at a cost of five dollars—I considered what I should do with the journal. One option was to take it to the county clerk's office. However, I decided to keep its location to myself, at least for the time being. I returned the volume to the lower shelf of the vault where Oliver and I found it, restacked the tax assessor records on top, and pushed back the boxes of office supplies to once again hide the shelf from view. And I left. I knew I was reacting to the frustration that it had taken me years to find the journal. It gave me comfort to know I was the only one, besides the disinterested Oliver, who knew its location, or even that it existed. However, on a subsequent visit I thought better of my decision and carried the journal from the planning vault upstairs to the country clerk's office, expecting to receive some praise for finding a journal the county clerk wasn't sure even existed. But other than a simple, "Thank you," there was none.

EVERY VISIT TO Wallowa County gained me new information, some significant, some of only passing interest, but I was always interested. And so, in early 2005, I visited again. I spoke with Charlotte McIver about Martin and the hidden records. McIver did not want to speak ill of Martin, and, by this time, neither did I. She praised Martin for devoting much of her life to the interests of Wallowa County and its people. She said that while Martin may have tucked away certain documents, to make them hard to find, she did it for what seemed the best of reasons—"She wanted to protect the interests of the county." And it wasn't just the county's reputation; she also wanted to protect the reputations of residents who were descendants of the members of the Evans gang. But McIver also knew that as a county clerk, Martin respected the integrity of public records and wouldn't have destroyed them.

McIver also revealed something I had not previously known, which was that Martin had worked with Harland Horner on his history and had typed his entire one thousand, six hundred-page manuscript, which Horner had written in longhand. So this completed the circle. Horner, Bartlett, and Martin had worked together to write the county's history, and they had written it the way they wanted it remembered.

THE LAST TIME I saw Marjorie Martin was on this same trip. Charlotte McIver had told me she was in bad shape. And so she was. A caregiver let me onto the screen porch, over which still sagged the broken gutter. She warned me that Martin, then ninety-one, was unable to speak, the result of several strokes. I found Marjorie—she was Marjorie now—sitting in one of her stuffed chairs, motionless, looking out the picture window into her backyard, seeing something or nothing. When I greeted her, her face was expressionless, but her eyes were glad to see me.

I initiated a largely one-sided conversation, telling her I was finishing my book and voicing appreciation for the information she had given me in the past. She tried to respond, but most of her words were unintelligible, except for one here and there. After ten minutes or so of struggling to make herself understood, Marjorie rose from her chair and touched my arm, motioning me to follow her. Stooped and with halting steps, she walked me to the coffee table at the far end of the room. As before, it was still strewn with scrapbooks, old documents, newspapers, and magazines. But there was more this time. Underneath and around the table, and stacked on nearby chairs, were loose papers, boxes stuffed with other papers, files, pictures, more newspapers, some new, some old. Marjorie rummaged through the documents, motioning me to take what I pleased, although nothing I saw had any obvious significance to the massacre. When she handed me a volume of *Life Magazine* photographs, I realized that to Marjorie, the papers and documents she had collected, coveted, and hidden over the years had become all the same.

Whenever I visited before, I had always come in search of information. And although this time I had come just to visit, she had it in her mind that I was still after information, and now, in her last years, she was willing to share everything. But I took nothing. I was polite about it. I didn't say I was confident I had already found nearly everything there was to find. Nor did I reveal I had discovered the trial journal, not wanting to disappoint her that she had been unable to keep it hidden, although I suspected she might not even remember it. I finally excused myself, telling Marjorie I would return another time, and if there was something she wanted me to see, to set it aside and I would get it then.

As I was leaving, her caregiver told me Marjorie spent a good part of every day going through her scrapbooks and papers, scattering them about. And if the caregiver tried to organize them, Marjorie would mix them up again.

This time, there was no good-by gem of a quote.

Martin died the next year, in 2006, at age ninety-two. McIver also died in 2006. She was sixty-five.

CHAPTER TWENTY-SEVEN

The Coffin Maker

HERMAN WEBB MADE the boxes out of galvanized sheet-metal. He remembered them as eight inches deep, ten inches wide, and twenty inches long. Webb, then employed by the Cook and Emele Sheet Metal Works of Baker City, made as many as forty boxes on special order from Gray's Western Funeral Parlor during the mid or late 1930s.

Then in his thirties, Webb didn't think much about the use to which the boxes would be put. "It was just another order and another job," he told me. But when the boxes were returned to be soldered shut, he was curious enough to lift the metal lid to look inside. There, amidst the packing material, he saw a human skull.[1]

BY THE 1930s, once-dynamic Chinatowns in interior cities like Baker City, John Day, and Lewiston had nearly disappeared. Other than menial work, few jobs remained for the Chinese; the placer mines were exhausted, the major railroads completed. A prosperous new economy had emerged around ranching and wheat, which largely excluded Chinese, except as hired hands. Most of the immigrant laborers had either returned to China or moved to larger cities, such as Portland, Seattle, or San Francisco.[2] However, there were a few, mostly elderly, who lived out their lives in the towns where they had come as young men. Webb remembered as a small boy seeing a Chinese peddler, known to whites by the demeaning name of "Old Humpy," who, with another Chinese, sold vegetables door-to-door in Baker City neighborhoods. "They had a big two-wheeled cart they pulled themselves."[3]

Today, even these last few are gone. Since they lived without women—except in rare instances—they left no descendants. The Chinatowns and their temples are long since demolished, replaced with development more useful to the white population.

The history of the Chinese in the interior of the Pacific Northwest is now largely lost. It was never kept. Chinese laborers, mostly illiterate and occupied by long hours of frequently back-breaking work, either weren't able to record their experiences, or weren't interested. And the whites among whom they lived focused on their own history. Of the Chinese experience, we are left with only fragments.

MARJORIE FONG, WHO died in 2000 at age eighty-eight, was the last direct link to Baker City's mining-era Chinese. The 1880 Census had listed Baker County's Chinese population at 787, including those clustered in the mining camps in the nearby Blue Mountains in places like Auburn, Sumpter, and Granite. Fong's parents were of the merchant class, who suffered fewer restrictions than laborers. They owned a mercantile store just down the block from Chinatown's two-story brick temple on Auburn Street. In a 1995 interview from her wheelchair—arthritis had ravaged her back—Fong became agitated when she recalled the time vandals ransacked the temple. A gang of "Caucasian hoodlums" had dragged a wooden Buddha into the street, where they chopped it to pieces. "I saw him all chopped up," Fong said, squirming with distress in her wheelchair.[4]

Fong also remembered how Caucasians mocked the Chinese practice of placing food on graves at the Qingming Festival, the spring observance when families clean and tend the graves of departed relatives. She said whites would sarcastically ask whether the bodies came up to eat the food. Her equally sarcastic reply: "Do your people come up and smell the flowers?"

Marjorie Fong, who died in 2000 at age eighty-eight, was the last direct link to Baker City's mining era Chinese. She grew agitated in an interview when recalling how a gang of "Caucasian hoodlums" dragged a wooden Buddha from the temple and chopped it to pieces. (Photo by the author)

A vegetable peddler in Mt. Idaho near Lewiston about 1920. After large-scale employment in gold mining and on railroads ended, the Chinese either left the interior towns of the Pacific Northwest or took whatever jobs were available. The Chinese were known for the quality of their vegetables and flowers. (Courtesy of Historical Museum at St. Gertrude, Cottonwood, Idaho)

Fong said Baker City wasn't a bad place for a young Chinese like herself to grow up—incidents were few. But she said most of the city's Chinese wanted to return to China. "That's all they thought about," she said. "Some saved enough money and went back, others didn't make it and were buried here."

Baker City's temple, built in 1882 at a cost to the Chinese of ten thousand dollars, was torn down years ago, replaced by a state office building.[5] All that is left of the city's Chinese history is the Chinese cemetery, located on what once was unwanted land near a city dump.

In Lewiston, not even the cemetery has survived. The city leased the land from the Chinese in 1891, and later turned it into a city park, called Prospect Park. It is on a bluff with a spectacular view overlooking the confluence of the Snake and Clearwater rivers and the wheat fields of eastern Washington. A sign notes the park's history as a cemetery, and the wish of the Chinese community that it always be "a pleasant place." Some, if not all, of the graves were moved to the newly established Chinese section of the city's main cemetery at Normal Hill.

The Chinese temple at Sixth and C streets was demolished in 1959 to clear the site for a new building for the *Lewiston Tribune*. The altar and many of its furnishings were preserved in a tasteful exhibit at the Lewis-Clark Center for Arts & History on Lewiston's Main Street until the center

Bodies of some of the murdered miners floated sixty-five miles from Deep Creek to Lewiston, where they were buried in the Chinese cemetery, now a city park. Whether the bodies are still buried here, or elsewhere, is unknown. (Photo by the author)

was damaged by fire in March 2009. The altar and furnishings sustained smoke damage, but were otherwise not seriously harmed. They have been removed to storage for repairs and to await a decision on future display.

Unlike the Lewiston cemetery, the Baker City cemetery escaped redevelopment because of its location on unwanted land—even today, it is separated from Baker City proper by Interstate 84. Over the years, as the Chinese community gradually dissolved, the cemetery succumbed to neglect, overgrown with sagebrush and littered with debris, forgotten even by the owner of the land, the Portland branch of the Chinese Six Companies, better known today by its legal name, the Chinese Consolidated Benevolent Association.[6]

Gloria Wong, a retired board member of the Portland CCBA, recalled her organization's surprise when it learned in 1991 that it owned the Baker City cemetery. A title search had revealed the ownership after a judge had awarded a portion of the unused property to a local businessman to widen a road. The CCBA reclaimed the property, after which it joined with the Baker County Historical Society in a project to renovate the cemetery.

Chinese-American students from Portland and other volunteers cleared the cemetery of refuse and brush. Volunteers surrounded it with a heavy chain fence and restored a stone prayer house—a six-foot-square structure used for burning prayer papers at the Qingming Festival and for other cemetery observances. Graded pathways lead through the sagebrush to dozens of indentations in the ground, formerly the graves of some of the nearly seventy Chinese once buried there, but no longer. The remains that Webb sealed in metal boxes came from these graves. The boxed remains were sent back to China. Webb died in 2007 at age ninety-eight.

The knowledge that their remains would be buried in their home villages was important to Chinese immigrants, reflecting the belief that their souls would wander endlessly if buried in a strange land, their graves untended by family.[7] The newly arrived Chinese typically paid a small fee to have their remains returned to China in the event of their death on American soil. The deceased were buried until their remains had decomposed, after which their bodies were disinterred and their bones were cleaned and packaged, and shipped home to China. The repatriation of remains, overseen by the CCBA, ended in the 1930s after the Japanese invaded China and was never resumed.

THERE IS NO record of the whereabouts of the bodies of the Chinese massacred in Hells Canyon. Those found at Deep Creek and elsewhere in the canyon were most likely buried in unmarked graves near where they were found. The rancher, George Craig, said he buried some of them. The *Lewiston Teller*, in its 1887 account of the initial discovery of the bodies in the river, said at least one was buried in Lewiston's Chinese cemetery. It's reasonable to assume other bodies found near Lewiston were buried there as well. Whether they were among those moved to the Normal Hill cemetery isn't known, as cemetery records make no mention of them. Possibly, they were repatriated to China. Lott Wiggins, the blacksmith whose shop burned in the 1883 fire that destroyed much of Lewiston's Chinatown, was the coffin maker for Lewiston's Chinese community.

It is, of course, possible that the bodies of the murdered miners were never moved, and remain today in the city park under the lush green grass now used for picnics and a playground, the "pleasant place."

CHAPTER TWENTY-EIGHT

Memorial Not

THERE IS NO satisfactory way to end an account of the massacre. Closure is impossible when there has been no manifestation of guilt, no expression of sorrow, no regret, no price paid, no consequences. All this was true when the massacre occurred, and remains true today.

The Nez Perce have received some acknowledgement of the crimes against them. While only a handful of Nez Perce live in Wallowa County today, the white population has adopted a facsimile of the Nez Perce legacy as its own, partly for its tourism potential, and partly—at least in recent years—to make amends. The town of Joseph hosts the annual Chief Joseph Days rodeo and parade, during which tribal members from several Northwest reservations ride in full regalia down Main Street, much to the delight of tourists—who have little awareness of the unhappy history.

Once called Silver Lake, or Lake City, Joseph was named for the Nez Perce chief in 1880, just three years after the expulsion of the Nez Perce. But although Chief Joseph's name is thus enshrined here, he was refused his request to return to the valley to live, although he did visit in 1899. He died in 1904, said to have succumbed to a broken heart, and is buried on the Colville Reservation at Nespelem, Washington.[1] Remains of his father, the elder Joseph, are buried under a monument on the moraine at the north end of Wallowa Lake. However, the old chief's skull is believed missing, stolen sometime before the body was moved from its original burial place near Lostine.

In the last few years, community and Nez Perce tribal leaders organized another and more serious celebration, called Tamkaliks. Held in mid-summer in the town of Wallowa at the opposite end of the valley from Joseph, the celebration is three days of dancing and feasting, which draws Native American dancers from throughout the Pacific Northwest. Tamkaliks, translated as "from where you can see the mountains," is a short distance from the Nez Perce's traditional main campsite near the junction of the Wallowa and Lostine rivers.

One of the founders of Tamkaliks was Earl "Taz" Conner, a Nez Perce I much admired, who traced his lineage to the young Chief Joseph. Conner's grandmother, Sarah, was the daughter of Ollokot, Joseph's younger brother, who was among those driven from the valley in 1877.[2] A decorated veteran, Conner died in 1999 at age sixty-one. By this time, both feet had been amputated, the result of the diabetes that ravaged his body.

WHILE RESIDENTS OF Wallowa County have taken some steps toward making amends for their ancestors' role in expelling the Nez Perce from their homeland, they have done nothing to address the other great crime in the county's history, the massacre of nearly three dozen Chinese gold miners. A cynic might surmise there is no tourism potential in the massacre. Or that perhaps the community wished not to open its eyes to a crime so ugly, so depraved, that it has had no near parallel in the county before or since. Such a cynic might also conclude that influential county residents want to avoid being reminded that the killers came from well-known families, some of whose descendants lived among them.

However, attitudes may be changing. A receptive audience of about eighty county residents attended a lecture I delivered on the massacre in Enterprise in February 2008.

SHORTLY AFTER THE discovery of the hidden documents in the old county safe, *Chieftain* editor Swart wrote an editorial that focused primarily on rectifying past abuses of the Nez Perce Indians. But he closed with this appeal.

The American people also need to make amends in some fashion with the people of China for the atrocities committed in the Chinese massacre of 1887. Ten to thirty Chinese miners were murdered and possibly tortured in Wallowa County's most heinous crime, a crime of bigotry and greed in an era when in the minds of most Euro-Americans the only thing worse than an Indian was a Chinaman. Not only did the crime go unpunished, the whole incident has been pretty much kept out of sight, out of mind for more than a century. For example, there is no memorial to the Chinese at Robinson Gulch [sic] documenting this historically significant event.

> *We would like to think the American people, champions of human*
> *rights around the globe, would want to recognize the sacrifices and*
> *contributions of other cultures in their own country as well.*[3]

Swart told me later he received virtually no community support for his suggested memorial, and none was built.

The U.S. Forest Service once maintained a sign acknowledging the massacre at Robinson Gulch, but removed it in the 1980s after it became a magnet for vandals and fortune hunters. Womack, the former Forest Service archaeologist, said the sign was poorly worded and wrongly placed, as the primary massacre site was Deep Creek.

Womack said he favored some kind of memorial to the Chinese victims, but the Forest Service declined to take the initiative for various reasons, including the controversy it might ignite among both Chinese Americans and residents of Wallowa County over the wording. He believed a memorial could be tastefully done, but would need community support, of which there was little—"There are some really weird feelings in this county."[4]

Given Wallowa County's long background of denial and refusal to address a grievous wrong, it should come as no surprise that even an innocuous proposal to mark the massacre site on maps of the region ran into strong opposition. The Oregon Geographic Names Board, meeting in June of 2004, wanted to designate a "Chinese Massacre Site" on official maps for a five-acre site where Deep Creek flows into the Snake River. But the board balked in the face of objections from the county. The Wallowa County Commission told the naming board in a letter dated May 19, 2004, it would prefer "an easily pronounced and spelled Chinese word or phrase that does honor to the victims and their contributions to the area's history without seeming to raise again, ill feelings and divisiveness."

The objection temporarily stalled the proposal, although it was resurrected in 2005 with a slightly different designation, "Chinese Massacre Cove." The county commission still objected, but the board approved the proposal nonetheless. The site designation was ratified by the United States Board on Geographic Names. Chinese Massacre Cove is now an official map designation, the first formal recognition by the federal government, or a government at any level, that the massacre actually occurred.

ON JUNE 27, 2008, I felt privileged to be among those in attendance when Nez Perce elder Horace Axtell led a healing ceremony for the Chinese miners on the banks of the Snake River at the newly named Chinese Massacre Cove. Axtell's participation was significant since the massacre site was once part of the vast Nez Perce homeland. The service was attended by about seventy-five people who had traveled by jetboat from Lewiston, retracing the same path taken by the Chinese miners one hundred and twenty-two years earlier. Speaking in both English and the Nez Perce language, Axtell said the Chinese had died with their spirits cleansed because their bodies had been thrown into the Snake River, considered sacred by the Nez Perce.

Nez Perce elder Horace Axtell, center, leads a healing ceremony at Chinese Massacre Cove. (Photo by the author)

CHAPTER TWENTY-NINE

Horner's Epilogue

HARLAND HORNER'S HISTORY of Wallowa County ends with a kind of epilogue, taken from a 1925 article in the *Chieftain*, then known as the *Enterprise Record Chieftain*.

Sheepherders Sugar Bowl Recalls Tragedy of Canyon

The new hand in the lambing camp on Deep Creek reached for the sugar bowl only to draw back in amazement when he found the container to be a human skull. Subsequent questioning brought out the story of the worst tragedy in the history of Wallowa County. The skull which had been picked up on a bar on Snake River, after having been washed out of a shallow grave, was that of a Chinaman, one of thirty-four who were foully murdered back in the '80s for a few thousand dollars worth of gold dust. After more than 30 years of buffeting by sand and water, a wandering sheepherder rescued the gruesome relic, and waggishly used it for a sugar bowl. There was a bullet hole in one side of the skull and the whole side of the head had apparently been blown away. In the rough and almost inaccessible wildness along Snake River, wild tales are told of an early day.

Around the campfires from a labor day in the hay fields, these old tales are recounted and made to live again. Although several thousand dollars in gold dust were found by the murderers, much of the treasure was never unearthed. Each apparently had a cache of his own, and thirty hiding places are difficult to find.

Twenty years after the tragedy a sheep herder found a small rusty baking powder can which had been washed out of a sand bank by the action of water. Curiosity impelled him to pick it up and he was startled to find it contained gold dust. The battered can yielded more than six hundred dollars worth of dust. The little hoard had cost a life.

The new lambing hand begged leave to carry away the grim reminder of that bygone day and has it for a curio. Meantime maintaining that some day, he is fully resolved to give this pitiful memento a decent burial.[1]

Epilogue

IN THE PROLOGUE to this book, I listed the names of eleven victims of the massacre at what is now officially known as Chinese Massacre Cove. I wanted to at least give these eleven some identity in the remembered history of the American West. It's not much. But it's something.

However, I've also wondered about the missing names, not just the names of the other victims of the massacre, but the names of the forgotten dead in other crimes against the Chinese. Who were the twenty-eight killed in the 1885 massacre at Rock Springs, Wyoming? Or the Chinese who perished while building the transcontinental railroad? Or the five Chinese hanged by vigilantes near Pierce, Idaho—we know the name of the white merchant they allegedly killed. With few exceptions, the Chinese victims of the white man's crimes were simply *Chinese* in the brief newspaper accounts and historical records—as if remaining nameless made their deaths less tragic. Would the names mean anything to us if we knew them? Probably not. But that's not the point.

The victims weren't unknown, of course. The Chinese government probably had their names. Surely their families in China learned of their fate. But I believe we would also benefit from knowing them. Even if we can't learn their names, we should be able to learn their stories. Our history books still have blank pages.

Knowing what I now know I'm certain there were crimes never investigated, never reported, and soon forgotten—whether because they were covered up, or simply because too many people didn't care. Some crimes may have been reduced to rumor. Were one hundred Chinese miners really buried alive at the Lily White mine, or was that story entirely contrived? Logic tells us something must be behind such a terrible rumor. Do we care enough now to want to know? How do we find out? Who finds out? It took nearly ten years of research before I felt I knew enough to write this book about the murdered Chinese in Hells Canyon. For me, it was worth the effort.

It goes without saying there are untold and unknown stories of crimes against others who were part of our history, especially Native Americans and African Americans. Their stories need telling more than they have been told so far.

It troubled me throughout my research that we know so little of the Chinese who lived and worked in the American West, although in recent years our knowledge has increased. Dedicated authors, historians, and volunteers are now working to learn what can be learned, save what can be saved, even if all that's left in some communities is an old overgrown Chinese cemetery. The bibliography with this book includes some of the recent work. There is more.

We owe the Chinese laborers a great deal. They helped build railroads, drained land, farmed crops. They prepared the land on which many of us now live. But their reward in the nineteenth century was too often mistreatment and abuse. The least we can do is fill the blank pages. We owe them their names.

Appendix

IN THE MONTHS following discovery of the massacre in Wallowa County, the well-known fiddler and former wagon-train captain, Isaac "Ike" Bare, composed a song about the crime that he sang and played at dances. There are several versions. As Horner knew Bare, his version is likely the most authentic. It is entitled "Old Blue."

OLD BLUE

It's not long since, I've learned by the laws of our land
That our law-abiding Citizens have taken in hand
A well-known Desperado, and horse brander too
He is known on the trails, as our Captain Old Blue.

So you had better stay at home Tommy, Don't go if you can
Stay close to your ranching, with your sweet Mary Ann
For there is Tighty so tricky and Omar so true
They will die on the trails for the life of Old Blue.

They brought him to justice. Bold action to try
And he thought for the present, his time was to die
For the N it was plain and the bar OK too
So they tried and bound over our Captain Old Blue.

Old Blue is an outlaw. And the Sheriff he stands
With a pair of cocked pistols, gripped tight in his hands
Now take a walk Tommy, I am telling you true
Take a walk for your health, and don't bother Old Blue.

Old Tighty is a night eagle. He rides on the trails
Equipments are graceful. He uses horse hides for sails
He's fond of wild life and he's a gold Buckeroo
But he failed to connect on the line with Old Blue.

He went down on Snake River. No horse could he find
And he thought of his dear friends, he'd left far behind.
His limbs they were wearing. And he was Durned [*sic*] hungry too
A prowling around on the trails for Old Blue.

There was Omar the ranger, he cared for no crime
Or for dear friends he had left far behind
He was fond of a wild life, and he was a wild brander too
But he failed to be there, at the last with Old Blue.

The Round House at Mackies, is filled every night
With Cow thieves and Bummers, with lips sealed tight
They run in wild horses, Nodines N makes an M
They drive to the Basin, known as Old Blue's den.

They ran the last cattle, the lean and the fat.
They roped and branded them on a long lonesome flat.
Old Snake River looked lonesome, No one was around.
The wind it was blowing, and no snow on the ground.

It was late in the evening when they brained the last man
And in fear, bid farewell to their Snake River land.
For the officers were coming, not for the men they slew.
And they took into custody, Their Captain Old Blue.

There was Tommy the orphan, he passed in his checks
For smearing fat cattle, too much around his lips.
But he gave it a chase, and he gave it in true
But he failed to connect, on the line with Old Blue.

So take a walk Tommy, Now don't go if you can,
Stay close to your ranch, with your sweet Mary Ann
For there is Tighty so tricky, and Omar so true.
Take a walk for your health, and don't follow Old Blue.[1]

THREE MEMBERS OF the Evans gang are mentioned: Old Blue, who is Evans; Tighty, who is J. T. Canfield, and Omar, who is Omar LaRue. "Mackie's" refers to the McMillan property, used as a gang hang-out. The frequent mention of "Tommy" refers to the boy victim, Tommy Harmon.

There was a reason Bare singled out Evans, Canfield, and LaRue for mention. They had fled the county, while the other gang members remained. As Bare performed at gatherings that almost certainly included friends, neighbors, even relatives of gang members, he probably wanted to avoid offending his audience. Bare also knew Frank Vaughan. He bought some of his land from Vaughan.

Significantly, Bare gave far more attention to the gang's rustling activities than to the massacre, which is mentioned only in passing and without even identifying the "brained" victims as Chinese. But he did note the irony that, although Evans thought he was being arrested for the murders, he was instead arrested for stealing horses.

ACKNOWLEDGMENTS

IN ADDITION TO Priscilla Wegars and David Stratton, both mentioned in the prologue, I am indebted to many others for their help and encouragement in writing this book. They include my wife, Candise; my late father and mentor, J. Richard Nokes; my son, Deston Nokes; my good friend and fellow explorer Mike Shanahan of Washington, D.C.; another good friend and author who encouraged me every step of the way, George Wright; Rich Wandschneider of Fishtrap in Enterprise; author Barry Lopez, who graciously read the manuscript; Jim Lynch, another author who gave of his time to read the manuscript; Lyle Wirtanen of the Historical Museum at St. Gertrude in Cottonwood, Idaho; Judge John Jelderks of Portland; Elane Dickenson of the Wallowa County Chieftain in Enterprise; Mary Leong of Beaverton and her late husband, George; Shawna Gandy, Eliza Canty-Jones, Marianne Keddington-Lang, and many others at the Oregon Historical Society; Donna Carnahan of Glenns Ferry, Idaho; Ann Hayes and the staff of the Wallowa County Museum in Joseph; Janet Jeffries of Boise and Kimberly England of Saratoga, California; Bill Rautenstrauch of La Grande; Richard Cockle, eastern Oregon correspondent for *The Oregonian*; Ben Boswell, Wallowa County commissioner; Richard Harris of Baker City; Greta Burles of the U.S. Forest Service in Baker City; Michael Brown of Cove; Bill Oliver of Enterprise; Diane Bradshaw of Lake Oswego; Warren Aney of Tigard; Lora Feucht of the Nez Perce County Historical Society in Lewiston; Martha Metcalf of the Josephine County Historical Society in Grants Pass; Elizabeth Gray of the National Archives at College Park, Maryland; Jayne Primrose of the Grant County Historical Museum in Canyon City; Gary Dielman of the Baker County Library; author Carole Simon-Smolinksi of Lewiston; author Craig Lesley; Bruce Womack of Enterprise; Gloria Wong of the Chinese Consolidated Benevolent Association in Portland; Jeff Ford of Boise; the late Gorden Lee of Milpitas, California; Joe and Donna Skovlin of Cove; Mark Highberger of Bear Creek Press in Wallowa; Rick Swart, formerly of the Chieftain; Dustin Fink of Glenns Ferry, Idaho; Tom Booth and Micki Reaman of Oregon State University and Jo Alexander, my patient editor at the press; as well as several people who are prominently mentioned in the book and are since deceased: Grace Bartlett, Charlotte McIver, Marjorie Martin, Majorie Fong, Vern Russell, Herman Webb, and Alvin Josephy. Any such list is incomplete, and to others whom I may have shamefully overlooked, my thanks to you, too.

Notes

PROLOGUE

1. Letter from Chang Yen Hoon, minister of the Chinese Legation in Washington, D.C., to Secretary of State Thomas F. Bayard, February 16, 1888, notes from the Chinese Legation to the United States, Department of State, 1868-1906, Microfilm M98, Record Group 59, National Archives Annex, College Park, MD. Also House Executive Documents, 2d Session, 50th Cong. 1888-'89, Vol. 1, Foreign Relations of the United States, 1888, Part 1, 383-84 .
2. Tentative identification by J. K. Vincent, U. S. Commissioner and Justice of the Peace for Nez Perce County, Idaho Territory, in written description of a body, dated July 8, 1887, enclosed with Chang to Bayard, February 16, 1888, House Executive Documents, 386.
3. Yung et al., *Chinese American Voices*, 1. The number is an estimate, and takes into account the two-way flow of immigrants—those who came and later returned to China. The largest official population of Chinese in the U.S. during the nineteenth century was 107,488 in the 1890 Census. It's unofficially estimated the total was about 132,000 before immigration restrictions took effect in 1882.

CHAPTER ONE

1. The name Hells Canyon wasn't in common use until the mid-twentieth century. Previously the canyon was known as Box Canyon or the Snake River Canyon. Carrey et al., *Snake River of Hells Canyon*, 2.
2. Findley, *Memoirs of Alexander B. and Sarah Jane Findley*, 130.
3. Carrey et al., *Hells Canyon*, 58.
4. Tucker, "Massacre for Gold," 26.

CHAPTER TWO

1. Bartlett, *The Wallowa Country*, 15. The survey was conducted by a team led by William H. Odell. Also, Josephy, *The Nez Perce Indians*, 439.
2. Circuit Court Grand Jury Indictment, March 23, 1888, *State of Oregon vs J. T. Canfield, Bruce Evans, L. O. LaRue, Hiram Maynard, Carl [sic] Hughes and Robert McMillan*. Records in County Clerk's vault, Wallowa County Courthouse, Enterprise, Oregon. Hereafter: Trial record.
3. Horner, *History of Wallowa County*, 307.
4. Ibid., 255.
5. *State of Oregon vs. J. T. Canfield*, information filed May 10, 1887; *State of Oregon vs. Bruce Evans*, information filed May 23, 1887. Trial record.
6. Horner, *History*, 414, 415. Douglas' name was spelled in some accounts as Douglass.
7. Findley, *Memoirs*, 129. Horner, *History*, 414.
8. Horner, *History*, 414.
9. Findley, *Memoirs*, 101.
10. Horner, *History*, 1371.
11. Ibid., 266, 267.
12. Trial record. Horner, *History*, 1227.
13. Horner, *History*, 256.
14. Trial record.
15. Trial record. Horner, *History*, 307.

16. Trial record.
17. Horner, *History*, 256.
18. Ibid., 1213.
19. Ibid., 940.
20. Findley, *Memoirs*, 130.
21. Ibid., 126, 128.
22. Ibid., 128.
23. Ibid., 130.
24. Ibid.
25. Ibid.
26. Horner, *History*, 732.

CHAPTER THREE

1. *Lewiston Teller*, June 16, 1887, 1. The words "Chinaman" or "Chinamen" are today considered racial slurs, although they were not always so considered by all who used them in the nineteenth century. Other names often used in a derogatory manner were Mongolians, Heathens, Tartars, and worse.
2. Ibid., June 30, 1887, 1.
3. Sung, *Story of the Chinese in America*, 12.
4. The Chinese Six Companies later grew to eight geographically based associations, although it maintained its original name. Chinn et al., *A History of the Chinese in California*, 66. Immigration records from this period were lost in the 1906 San Francisco earthquake and fire, which destroyed much of that city's original Chinatown. The U.S. Census didn't always identify Chinese by name. The simple description "A Chinaman" appears frequently on Census lists.
5. Chen, *A Gold Dream*, 69. Chen cites an old saying, "Although our blood is not close, our lands are."
6. Anonymous, "From the Orient Direct," *The Atlantic Monthly*, November, 1869, 542.
7. Matthews, *American Merchant Ships*, 44-47. The ship's transport of Chinese laborers ended with the ban on immigration of Chinese laborers in 1882; it subsequently carried general cargo. After later being converted to a coal barge, it foundered in an Atlantic gale, taking down her captain and a crew of three.
8. Among ships docking in Portland with their cargoes of Chinese that year were the American barks *Garibaldi*, carrying 210 Chinese, and the *Edward James*, 380; and the French ship, *Jennie Alice*, with 430. Ho, *Portland's Chinatown*, 7, 10.
9. Feichter, *Chinese Culture*, 203. Representatives of the Chinese Six Companies made occasional trips to gravesites throughout the West to collect the bones of deceased Chinese.
10. Chinn et al., *Chinese in California*, 13.
11. Ambrose, *Nothing Like it in the World*, 153.
12. Allen, *Lewiston Country*, 10. Allen wrote that Lewiston's population "fluctuated like the tide" because of mining activity with estimates in its first few years ranging from twelve thousand to as low as 365. Josephy, in *The Nez Perce Indian*, put Lewiston's population at two thousand in 1862, quoting a report by Edward Giddings, chief clerk of the Surveyor General's Office in the Washington Territory.
13. Allen, *Lewiston Country*, 41.
14. Ibid., 123.

15. Wegars, *Chinese of the Confluence*, 3.
16. Ibid., 4. Wegars cites an article in the 1961 *Lewiston Morning Tribune* quoting a February 1865 article in the defunct *North-Idaho Radiator* that "some thirty Chinese arrived in Lewiston the past week, who are said to be merely the advance guard of several hundreds of the race, now en route to the Northwest portion of Idaho for the purpose of working the poorer class of mines."
17. Chinese generally weren't allowed to establish claims, but could buy them from whites.
18. Tsai, *The Chinese Experience in America*, 10.
19. Chinn et al., *Chinese in California*, 32, 33.

CHAPTER FOUR

1. Tsai, *Chinese Experience*, 33.
2. Ibid., 57.
3. This figure was compiled by Coolidge, *American Public Problem*, 498. It is generally accepted by Chinese-American historians.
4. Tsai, *China and the Overseas Chinese*, 21.
5. Ibid., 15, 16. Also, Chinn et al., *Chinese in California*, 11.
6. Sung, *Story of the Chinese*, 11.
7. Chinn et al., *Chinese in California*, 11.
8. Chinese also emigrated to the Hawaiian Islands, Cuba, Peru, and other countries in Latin America.
9. www.wikipedia.org/wiki/taiping_rebellion.
10. Chinn et al., *Chinese in California*, 11.
11. Tsai, *Overseas Chinese*, 10, 14. Guangdong Province is one hundred and twelve thousand square miles to Oregon's ninety-six thousand square miles.
12. Chinn et al., *Chinese in California*, 12.
13. Ibid., 44. The authors report that four of every five hires by the Central Pacific were Chinese.
14. Tsai, *Chinese Experience*, 17. Also, Ambrose, *Nothing Like It*, 157.
15. Tsai, *Overseas Chinese*, 13. Chinn et al., *Chinese in California*, 16, 47.
16. Tsai, *Chinese Experience*, 8.
17. Chinn et al., *Chinese in California.*, 47.
18. Ibid., 45.
19. Unsigned and undated letter found with other letters at the Kam Wah Chung store in John Day, Oregon. Translation in 1974 by Chia-lin Chen. Letters on file at the Oregon Historical Society Research Library in Portland. Many of the laborers were illiterate and paid "letter-writers" wrote their letters.
20. Lewiston's "A" Street washed away in a flood years earlier, and the alphabetical street grid continued to begin with "B" until 2008, when the street names were changed. Wegars, *Chinese at the Confluence*, 8.
21. *An Illustrated History of North Idaho*, 111.
22. Day, *Lewiston Country*, 125. Also, Elsensohn, *Idaho Chinese Lore*, 16. Both authors report that the fire destroyed a temple. However, Priscilla Wegars, volunteer curator of the Asian American Comparative Collection at the University of Idaho, wrote in her study of Lewiston temples that the fate of one or more early temples dating to 1875 is uncertain. Wegars said newspaper coverage of the 1883 fire made no mention of a temple and, moreover, that the fire was well away from the temple location. Wegars, *Beuk Aie Temple*, 12, 13.
23. Ibid., 13, 18, 38. The contributions were in amounts from twenty-five cents to fifteen dollars; the six women contributed between fifty cents and five dollars.

24. Wegars, *Beuk Aie Temple*, 13. The deities are listed here as Beuk Aie, God of the North and the deity for water and flood control; Toy Guon, God of Riches; Wah Ho, God of Medicine; Quon Yim, Goddess of Mercy; and Kuan Kung, God of Brotherhood, Fairness and Loyalty; they were also known by other names, titles and honors.

25. A temple in Weaverville, California, built in 1884 and visited by the author in July of 2007 is maintained in excellent condition by California State Parks. It features separate altars and images for all three beliefs: Daoist, Confucian, and Buddhist.

CHAPTER FIVE

1. Findley, *Memoirs*, 2, 8, 9.
2. Ibid., 223, 224.
3. Ibid., 130.
4. Ibid.
5. Horner, *History*, 1,210.
6. Ibid.
7. Horner, *History*, 270, and deposition of Hiram Maynard, given in State of Oregon, County of Wallowa, vs. Bruce Evans, J. T. Canfield, C. O. Omar LaRue, Robert McMillan, H. K. Hughes and H. Maynard, April 16, 1888. Trial record.
8. Horner, *History*, 270.
9. Ibid., 256.
10. Stratton, "The Snake River Massacre," 117.
11. *An Illustrated History of Union and Wallowa Counties*, 486.

CHAPTER SIX

1. Vincent was U.S. commissioner for the Lewiston district. He was also the elected justice of the peace for Nez Perce County. His legal documents were signed with one or the other of the titles, and sometimes both.
   According to the Hon. Leslie G. Foschio, the position of U.S. commissioner was quasi-judicial, appointed by a district or circuit court judge and authorized to hear evidence in federal and civil cases, issue arrest warrants, and adjudicate misdemeanor and certain other crimes. The position evolved into today's U.S. magistrate judge. It wasn't unusual for a U.S. commissioner to hold one or more other positions, even political office, which gave rise to criticism and eventual reform. The U.S. commissioner was paid according to a uniform fee schedule for work performed. Foschio, "Development of the Office of United States Commissioner," 1.
2. Vincent to Liang Ting Tsan, Chinese consul-general in San Francisco, and F. A. Bee, consul, July 19, 1887, enclosed with Chang Yen Hoon to Thomas F. Bayard, February 16, 1888, House Executive Documents, 385.
3. Stratton, "Snake River Massacre," 119.
4. Amount of reward in Tucker, "Massacre for Gold," 27. Also reference to reward in Chang to Bayard, February 16, 1888, House Executive Documents, 385.
5. *Illustrated History of North Idaho*, 571.
6. Ibid.
7. Ibid., 99, 100.
8. Ibid., 571.
9. *Idaho County Free Press*, Grangeville, Idaho, March 25, 1909, 3.

10. *Lewiston Teller*, June 8, 1886.
11. *Idaho County Free Press*, March 25, 1909, 3.
12. *Lewiston Morning Tribune*, May 14, 1961.
13. *History of North Idaho*, 41.

CHAPTER SEVEN
1. Greta Burles, District Geologist, Wallowa-Whitman National Forest, Baker City, Oregon, e-mail to author, Dec. 2, 2008.
2. Horner, *History*, 270.
3. National Forest Recreation Survey, *Site of 1887 Chinese Massacre*, 1960, Supervisor's Office, Wallowa-Whitman National Forest, Federal Building, Baker City, Oregon; copy in possession of author. Hereafter: Forest Service survey.
4. Warren W. Aney, former Northeast Region Supervisor for the Oregon Department of Fish and Wildlife, took the pictures at the site in 1980.
5. Forest Service survey.
6. Ibid.
7. The entry was a photocopy of typescript in a scrapbook at the Copper Creek Lodge. It carried the notation, Volume 111. Jim Pencil Pusher. Further Chronicles of James Brewrink 1928-1938. This and additional pages were also sent to the author by Carole Simon-Smolinksi of Lewiston.

CHAPTER EIGHT
1. Telephone interviews September 2001 and March 5, 2009.
2. James, *Ruins of a World*, 13.
3. Ibid., 30.
4. Ibid., 24-29.
5. Ibid.
6. Wegars, *Uncovering a Chinese Legacy*, 19. Their names were Hung Dye, Hung Hang, Joe Dot, Ah Ty, and Ah Sing.
7. Ibid.
8. Horner, *History*, 314.
9. *History of North Idaho*, 83.
10. The Gin Lin Trail is in the Applegate Ranger District in the Rogue River-Siskiyou National Forest about fifteen miles south of Jacksonville, Oregon. www.fs.fed.us/r6/rogue-siskiyou/recreation/trails.
11. Day, *Lewiston Country*, 124.
12. *Asian Americans in Oregon*, 8.

CHAPTER NINE
1. Trial record.
2. Complaint signed by Lee Loi against unknown killers of ten Chinese, July 8, 1887, enclosed with Chang to Bayard, February 16, 1888. House Executive Documents, 386.
3. Vincent to Liang, July 19, 1887, enclosed with Chang to Bayard, February 16, 1888. House Executive Documents, 385.
4. Tucker, "Massacre for Gold."
5. Ibid.
6. Vincent to Governor E. A. Stevenson, April 14, 1888. Miscellaneous Letters of the State Department, 1789-1906. Microfilm M179, Record Group 59, National Archives Annex, College Park, Maryland. Hereafter: Letters of State Department.

CHAPTER TEN

1. Tsai, *Overseas Chinese*, 26. Attracting more laborers was a U.S. goal of the treaty.
2. Treaties and Other International Agreements of the United States of America, 684.
3. Sung, *Chinese in America*, 47, 48.
4. Tsai, *Overseas Chinese*, 38.
5. Ibid., 51.
6. Coolidge, *American Public Problems*, 86, 87. Coolidge wrote that the Senate committee report was widely circulated and used to support a move in Congress to prohibit Chinese immigration.
7. But not everyone felt this way. Among others, many clergy and employers, including households who employed Chinese as domestics, resisted the movement.
8. Chinn et al., *Chinese in California*, 24.
9. Pfaelzer, *Driven Out*, 47.
10. Treaties and Other International Agreements, 685.
11. 1882 Exclusion Act, 47th Congress, Session I, 1882.

CHAPTER ELEVEN

1. Tsai, *Chinese Experience*, 65.
2. Ibid., 19.
3. For an excellent account of the activities aimed at driving Chinese from towns throughout northern California, see Pfaelzer, *Driven Out*.
4. Tsai, *Chinese Experience*, 83.
5. Ibid., 71.
6. While Chinese laborers typically immigrated without their wives, merchants and professionals frequently did bring wives and families.
7. Pfaelzer, *Driven Out*, 222.
8. Ibid., 67.
9. *The Oregonian*, February 7, 1886, 2.
10. Ibid., February 9, 1886, 1.
11. Ibid.
12. Statement of Claims, sent with Chang to Bayard, March 3, 1888, House Executive Documents, 390-92.
13. Letter from San Francisco Consul General Owyang Ming to Chinese Legation, Oct. 9, 1885, Notes from the Chinese Legation. Also, Elsensohn, *Chinese Lore*, 29, 30.
14. Letter dated April 15, 1885. Notes from the Chinese Legation.
15. *The Oregonian*, February 14, 1886, 2.
16. MacColl, *Merchants, Money and Power*, 238-42.
17. *The Oregonian*, February 17, 1886, 2.
18. Ibid., February 18, 1886, 2.
19. Ibid., February 23, 1886, 2.
20. Ibid., February 24, 1886.
21. Ibid., March 5, 1886, 2.
22. Ibid., March 13, 1886, 2.
23. Ibid., March 11, 1886.
24. Ibid., March 17, 1886, 2.
25. Ibid.

26. Ibid., March 25, 1886, 2.

27. Ho, *Portland's Chinatown*, 10.

28. Nokes, *Keeping the Lily White*.

29. Telephone interview, September 1995.

30. Ibid. Harris protested when the Forest Service removed one sign alluding to the rumored atrocity, with the result that the Forest Service put up a new sign. Harris recovered the original sign and posted it over his garage in Baker City, where it remained in 2009.

31. Telephone interview, February 11, 2009.

32. Chen, *A Gold Dream*, 112.

33. Memorial of Chinese Laborers, Resident at Rock Springs, Wyoming Territory, to the Chinese consulate at New York (1885), read on the George Mason University website, www.historymatters.gmu.edu. Also, Yung et al., *Chinese American Voices*, 52.

34. Pfaelzer, *Driven Out*, 211.

CHAPTER TWELVE

1. Cheng to Bayard, February 15, 1886. Notes from the Chinese Legation.

2. Biographical information on Bayard from http://en.wikipedia.org/wik/ Thomas_F._Bayard.

3. Tansill, *The Foreign Policy of Thomas F. Bayard,* 134.

4. Bayard to Cheng, February 18, 1886. Notes from the Chinese Legation.

5. *The Oregonian*, March 3, 1886, 1.

6. Ibid.

7. Chang to Bayard, February 16, 1888. House Executive Documents, 383-84.

8. Ibid.

9. Ibid.

10. Ibid.

11. Bayard to Chang, Feb. 23, 1888. House Executive Documents, 387, 388.

CHAPTER THIRTEEN

1. Trial record.

2. Findley, *Memoirs*, 131.

3. *New York Times*, April 29, 1888, 1. The article was probably a pickup from the *Walla Walla Weekly Union*, which carried a nearly identical article the previous day.

4. Rautenstrauch, "A Skeleton in the Closet," 22.

5. McArthur, *Oregon Geographic Names*, 771.

6. Ibid., 384.

7. Josephy, *The Nez Perce*, 14. Josephy wrote that the tribe was one of the "more numerous and powerful" in the Pacific Northwest.

8. Ibid., xiv, 9.

9. Nez Perce official Web site, www.nezperce.org, says that the name Nez Perce was given by an interpreter with the Lewis and Clark expedition in 1805.

10. Josephy, *The Nez Perce*, 401. Josephy quotes the Giddings report that, by 1862, some 18,690 whites lived on Nez Perce land, including 2,000 in Lewiston, 3,514 in Pierce City, and 9,200 in Florence.

11. Ibid., 419, 420.

12. Bartlett, *Wallowa Country*, 13.

13. Josephy, *The Nez Perce*, 442, 647, 437. Josephy estimated the 1860 population of the Wallowa band at sixty men and "possibly twice that many women

and children." Findley gave a slightly higher estimate of seventy men, plus women and children, *Memoirs*, 32. The Nez Perce' tribal Web site (www.wallowanezperce.org) gives no estimate.

14. Josephy, 438. He estimated there were five hundred settlers in the Grande Ronde Valley in 1864.

15. Bartlett, *Wallowa Country*, 17, 18, 31. Names of the settlers on 85-88.

16. Josephy, *The Nez Perce*, 448-51.

17. Bartlett, *Wallowa Country*, 16. Also www.ourdocuments.gov/doc.

18. Findley, *Memoirs*, 36. Also, Josephy, *The Nez Perce*, 461.

19. Josephy, *The Nez Perce*, 458, 494.

20. Ibid., 494.

21. Bartlett, *Wallowa Country*, 70-71.

22. Josephy, *The Nez Perce*, 496-98.

23. Ibid., 498, 501.

24. Ibid., 609. Although Wood claimed to have recorded Joseph's speech in writing as it was translated to him, the on-line encyclopedia of Oregon history, www.oregonencyclopedia.org, said Wood's account is not without controversy: "Wood claimed to have written it down as Joseph spoke, but some historians believe that Wood recorded a speech Joseph gave to his chiefs in council as reported to Wood by two Nez Perce go-betweens." Schlesier said the Wood translation can't be accurate because Wood didn't understand Nez Perce and no interpreter was present at the surrender. *Aurora Crossing*, 372.

25. Josephy, *The Nez Perce*, 612.

26. Schlesier wrote that 233 Nez Perce escaped from Bear Paw. *Aurora Crossing*, 372.

CHAPTER FOURTEEN
1. Author's first interview with Boswell, July 13, 1995.

2. Nokes, "The terrible secret," 1.

3. Interview July 24, 2001, and telephone interview, Aug. 3, 2001.

4. Trial record.

CHAPTER FIFTEEN
1. Trial record. Vaughan deposition.

2. Ibid., McMillan deposition.

3. Horner, *History*, 254

4. Ibid., 567.

CHAPTER SIXTEEN
1. *Wallowa County Chieftain*, April 19, 1888, from a copy obtained by the author from the personal files of Marjorie Martin, a former Wallowa County clerk.

2. Ibid.

3. Trial record.

4. Ibid.

5. Ibid.

CHAPTER SEVENTEEN
1. Letter from James Slater to L.L. McArthur, April 24, 1888, House Executive Documents, 402.

2. *Asian Americans in Oregon*, 8.

3. Ibid.

4. McArthur to U.S. Attorney General A. H. Garland, April 28, 1888, National Archives and Records Service, Reference Service Report, May 4, 1961. Also Tsai, *Overseas Chinese*, 86. Also McArthur to Secretary of State Bayard, April 28, 1888, Letters of the State Department.
5. Tsai, *Overseas Chinese*, 86.
6. Acting Secretary of State G. L. Rives to Chang, May 15, 1888. House Executive Documents, 401, 402.
7. Chang to Bayard, May 20, 1888. House Executive Documents, 403.
8. Vincent to Governor E. A. Stevenson, April 14, 1888. Letters of the State Department.
9. Stevenson to Bayard, April 19, 1888. Ibid.
10. A copy of Stevenson's proclamation pledging protection of the Chinese was reprinted in the *Asian American Comparative Collection Newsletter,* Laboratory of Anthropology, University of Idaho, Moscow, Idaho (March 2006).

CHAPTER EIGHTEEN

1. There were a few instances where Caucasians were punished for crimes against Chinese, although the exceptions often proved the rule. Pfaelzer wrote that eight white men were sent to San Quentin prison for terms of two to six years for manslaughter in connection with the lynching of seventeen Chinese in Los Angeles in 1871. However, within months, the verdict was reversed and the men released. *Driven Out*, 53.
2. This is the hanging incident at Pierce, mentioned earlier in the text.
3. Letter from Chang to Bayard, March 3, 1888. House Executive Documents, 390-92. In the *Virginius* case, the United States sought indemnity from Spain after the Spanish Navy seized a ship called *Virginius* in 1873 and executed fifty-one crew members and passengers, Americans among them. As part of the settlement, Spain paid an indemnity of $80,000 to the United States that included compensation for the slain Americans.
4. Ibid., 392.

CHAPTER NINETEEN

1. Building history from Wallowa Title Company news release in possession of author.
2. Findley, *Memoirs*, 131.
3. Horner, *History*, 1232.
4. Trial record.
5. Ibid.
6. Court Docket, 1888-1898, entry for September 7, 1888, County Clerk's vault, Wallowa County Courthouse, Enterprise, Oregon. Hereafter: Court Docket.
7. Trial record.
8. Notes from an interview with George S. Craig, March 2, 1936, Works Progress Administration, Historical Records Survey, Oregon Records BX 66-30, in Special Collections, University of Oregon Library, Eugene, Oregon.
9. Ibid.
10. Stratton, "Snake River Massacre," 125.
11. Tucker, "Massacre for Gold," Fall, 1961.
12. Ben Weathers column, *Wallowa County Chieftain*, Aug. 4, 1966, collection of Weathers' columns, Wallowa County Museum, Joseph, Oregon.
13. Ibid.

CHAPTER TWENTY
1. *State of Oregon vs. Bruce E. Evans.* Trial record.
2. Findley, *Memoirs*, 131.
3. Horner, *History*, 257.
4. Ibid., 1212.
5. Ibid., 1213.

CHAPTER TWENTY-ONE
1. Tsai, *Overseas Chinese*, 89-91.
2. MacColl, *Merchants, Money and Power*, 239.
3. Senate debate as reported in *The Morning Oregonian*, Portland, Oregon, September 8, 1888, p. 1.
4. Mitchell, who had a checkered career, was convicted of land fraud in 1905 and sentenced to six months in jail and fined one thousand dollars; he died that same year before his appeal of the sentence could be heard. Land Fraud Trial of Senator John Mitchell, Oregon History Project, www.ohs.org/education/oregonhistory.
5. Tsai, *Overseas Chinese*, 91.
6. Letter from Rives to Chang, October 19, 1888. Notes from the Chinese Legation.
7. Tsai, *Overseas Chinese*, 82.

CHAPTER TWENTY-TWO
1. *Walla Walla Statesman*, Walla Walla, Washington, September 30, 1891, p. 3.
2. Ibid.
3. *Wallowa County Chieftain*, Joseph, Oregon, October 8, 1891, typewritten copy sent to the author by David Stratton.
4. Ibid.
5. The first reference I found to thirty-four victims appeared April 26, 1888, in the *Lewiston Teller*, quoting on p. 2 an earlier article in the *Wallowa Signal*. The *Teller* was skeptical, however: "Who knows that any thirty-four Chinamen went on to any such bar and went to mining last fall. We discredit the story and shall do so until further evidence be made manifest."
6. Stratton, "Snake River Massacre," 113. A greater number of Chinese may have been killed by Native Americans. Stratton wrote that between forty and sixty Chinese were killed along the Owyhee River in southeastern Oregon by a band of Paiutes in 1866. A similar account is in Michno, *The Deadliest Indian War in the West*, 152. Michno wrote that forty-nine of a party of fifty Chinese were killed by Paiutes, led by Chief Egan, along the Owyhee River on May 19, 1866.

CHAPTER TWENTY-THREE
1. Copy of article from *Oregon Scout*, Union, Oregon, July 20, 1888.
2. Horner, *History*, 417.
3. Ibid., 271.
4. Ibid.
5. Findley, *Memoirs*, 130.
6. Horner, *History*, 417.
7. Ibid.
8. Ibid.
9. Ibid., 416.

CHAPTER TWENTY-FOUR

1. Findley, *Memoirs*, 224.
2. *Gone But Not Forgotten*, 57.
3. Findley, *Memoirs*, 224.
4. Photographs from files of the *Wallowa County Chieftain*.
5. Findley, *Memoirs*, 226.
6. Horner, *History*, 1212.
7. Interview by author, July 13, 1995.
8. Findley, *Memoirs*, 234.
9. Horner, *History*, 1213.
10. Elsensohn, *Pioneer Days in Idaho County*, 182-83.
11. Horner, *History*, 1213.
12. Telephone interview October 5, 2004.
13. Telephone interview October 8, 2004.
14. Horner, *History*, 1212. Horner said McMillan "took sick and died"' at a hospital in Walla Walla, but didn't mention the illness. However, diptheria is a possibility, as the illness devastated many families in the region. Findley wrote in his *Memoirs* that his parents, Alexander and Sarah Jane Findley, lost six children to the illness, 64.
15. Stratton, "Snake River Massacre," 123.
16. Horner, *History*, 1213.
17. Wikipedia classifies Mt. Idaho as a ghost town.
18. Horner, *History*, 1229.
19. Oregon History Project of the Oregon Historical Society, www.ohs.org/ education/oregonhistory/historical_records

CHAPTER TWENTY-FIVE

1. Telephone interview September 2001.
2. Interview July 12, 1995. Quotations previously used in Nokes, "Terrible secret."
3. Interview July 13, 1995.
4. Letters column, *Wallowa County Chieftain*, February 1995.
5. Bartlett, *From the Wallowas*, 61.
6. Ibid., 58.
7. Grace Bartlett's personal background was confirmed by the author with family members.
8. Bartlett, *Wallowa Country*, 12.
9. Telephone interview April 10, 2001.

CHAPTER TWENTY-SIX

1. Circuit Court Journal, Volume A, 1887-1893, August 30, 1888. County Clerk's vault, Wallowa County Courthouse, Enterprise, Oregon, 78.
2. Ibid., September 1, 1888, 80.
3. Ibid., March 22, 1888, 39.

CHAPTER TWENTY-SEVEN

1. Interview October 16, 1995.
2. Chen, *Gold Dream*, p. 112. Chen wrote that the Chinese government decided in 1906 to provide free passage home for Chinese laborers who were elderly, disabled, or ill. But he said not all took advantage of this offer.
3. Interview October 16. 1995.

4. Interview October 16. 1995.

5. Andrews, "Baker City in the 1880s," 87-89.

6. The CCBA maintains its national headquarters at 843 Stockton Street in San Francisco's Chinatown, where three large stone lions guard the front steps leading to the building's ornate gold, red, and green entrance. The organization shouldered much of the cost of rebuilding San Francisco's Chinatown after it was largely destroyed in the fire that followed the 1906 earthquake. With fewer official duties today, the CCBA organizes festivals and provides social and educational centers for Chinese communities in major American cities. One of their most important functions is to offer Chinese language classes to Chinese-American children.

7. Tsai, *Chinese Experience*, 10.

CHAPTER TWENTY-EIGHT

1. Josephy, *The Nez Perce*, 625.

2. Interview July 17, 1996. Also, www.mail-archive.com/nativenews@mlists.net

3. Swart, *Wallowa County Chieftain*, July 6, 1995, 4.

4. Telephone interview September 2001.

CHAPTER TWENTY-NINE

1. Horner, *History*, 1232-33.

APPENDIX

1. Horner, *History*, 254-55.

Bibliography

Allen, Margaret Day, *Lewiston Country* (Lewiston, Idaho: Nez Perce County Historical Society, 1990).

Ambrose, Stephen E., *Nothing Like it in the World, The Men Who Built the Transcontinental Railroad, 1863-1869* (New York: Simon and Schuster, 2000)

Andrews, Wesley, "Baker City in the 1880s," *Oregon Historical Quarterly*, Volume 50, 1949.

Asian Americans in Oregon (Oregon State University Extension Service and Oregon Agricultural Experiment Station, in cooperation with Oregon Department of Education, Salem, Oregon, September 1990).

Bartlett, Grace, *The Wallowa Country, 1867-1877* (Fairfield, Washington: Ye Galleon Press, 1984).

Bartlett, Grace, *From the Wallowas* (Enterprise, Oregon: Pika Press, 1992).

Brewrink, James, *The Chronicles of James Brewrink*, undated and unpublished memoir provided to author by Carole Simon-Smolinksi.

Brott, Clark W., *Moon Lee One: Life in Old Chinatown Weaverville, California* (Redding, California: prepared under contract with North Valley Bank, Redding, 1982).

Carrey, Johnny, Cort Conley, and Ace Barton, *Snake River of Hells Canyon* (Cambridge, Idaho: Backeddy Books, 1979).

Chen, Chia-lin, *A Gold Dream in the Blue Mountains, A Study of the Chinese Emigration in the John Day Area, 1870-1910* (M.A. thesis, Portland State University, 1972).

Chen, Chia-lin (translator and compiler), *Kam Wah Chung Co., John Day, Oregon, Papers*, a volume of letters (Portland: Oregon Historical Society archives, 1974).

Chinn, Thomas W., Him Mark Lai, and Philip P. Choy, *A History of the Chinese in California, A Syllabus* (San Francisco: Chinese Historical Society of America, 1969).

Coolidge, Mary Roberts, *American Public Problems, Chinese Immigration* (New York: Henry Holt & Co., 1909).

Craig, George S., notes from an interview, March 2, 1936, Works Progress Administration, Historical Records Survey, Oregon Records BX 66-30, in Special Collections, University of Oregon Library, Eugene.

Dirlik, Arif, with Malcolm Yeung, *Chinese on the American Frontier* (Lanham, Maryland: Rowman & Littlefield, 2001).

Doermer, Diane, Ladd Hamilton, and Johnny Johnson, *Historic Downtown Lewiston, A Self-guided Walking Tour* (Lewiston, Idaho: Nez Perce County Historical Society, undated).

Elsensohn, Sister M. Alfreda, *Idaho Chinese Lore* (Cottonwood, Idaho: Corporation of Benedictine Sisters, 1993).

Elsensohn, Sister M. Alfreda, Pioneer Days in Idaho County (Cottonwood, Idaho: Corporation of Benedictine Sisters, 2 volumes, 1971).

Feichter, Nancy, "Chinese Culture in the Inland Empire," in *Chinese on the American Frontier*, edited by Arif Dirlik (Lanham, Maryland: Rowman & Littlefield, 2001).

Findley, H. R., Memoirs of Alexander B. and Sarah Jane Findley, Book 2 (series in the *Chief Joseph Herald* October 24, 1957-February 24, 1959; concluded in the *Wallowa County Chieftain*, March 12, 1959-February 4, 1960. A copy is in possession of the author and used with permission of the Findley family).

Foschio, Leslie G., A History of the Development of the Office of United States Commissioner and Magistrate Judge System, *Federal Courts Law Review*, 4, 1999.

Gone But Not Forgotten, The Pioneers of the I.O.O.F. Cemetery, Joseph, Oregon, Their Lives and Times (compiled by the Hurricane Creek Grange, 1998).

Highberger, Mark, *Snake River Massacre* (Wallowa, Oregon: Bear Creek Press, 1997).

Ho, Nelson Chia-Chi, *Portland's Chinatown, The History of an Urban Ethnic District* (Portland, Oregon: Bureau of Planning, City of Portland, 1978).

Horner, J. Harland, *History of Wallowa County* (unpublished, Oregon Historical Society Library, Portland).

House Executive Documents, 2d Session, 50th Congress, 1888-1889, Vol 1. Correspondence of J. K. Vincent, U.S. commissioner and justice of the peace for Nez Perce County, Idaho Territory, and correspondence between China's Chief of Legation Chang Yen Hoon and Secretary of State Thomas F. Bayard.

Hui, Huang, "Overseas Studies and the Rise of Foreign Cultural Capital in Modern China," *International Sociology* (Palo Alto, California: Sage Publications, 2002) 17:35-55. http://iss.sagepub.com/cgi/reprint/17/1/35

An Illustrated History of Union and Wallowa Counties, History of Wallowa County, Parts I and II (San Francisco: Western Historical Publishing Co., 1902 and 1903).

James, Ronald L., *Ruins of a World, Chinese Gold Mining at the Mon-Tung Site in the Snake River Canyon* (U. S. Department of the Interior, Bureau of Land Management: Idaho Cultural Series Number IV, 1995).

Josephy, Alvin M. Jr., *The Nez Perce Indians and the Opening of the Northwest*, Abridged Edition (Lincoln and London: University of Nebraska Press, 1971).

Lewiston Teller, Lewiston, Idaho Territory, June 16 and June 30, 1887.

MacColl, E. Kimbark, *Merchants, Money and Power, The Portland Establishment, 1843-1913* (Portland, Oregon: The Georgian Press, 1988).

Matthews, Frederick C., *American Merchant Ships, 1850-1900* (New York: Dover Publications, 1987).

McArthur, Lewis A., *Oregon Geographic Names, Fifth Edition* (Portland: Western Imprints, The Press of the Oregon Historical Society, 1982), 771.

Memorial of Chinese Laborers, resident at Rock Springs, Wyoming Territory, to the Chinese consulate at New York (1885).

Michno, Gregory, *The Deadliest Indian War in the West: The Snake Conflict, 1864-1868* (Caldwell, Idaho: Caxton Press, 2007).

Nokes, R. Gregory, "Keeping the Lily White gold-mine story alive," *The Oregonian*, December 21, 1995, C2.

Nokes, R. Gregory, " 'A Most Daring Outrage': Murders at Chinese Massacre Cove, 1887," *Oregon Historical Quarterly*, Fall, 2006, 326.

Nokes, R. Gregory, "The terrible secret of Hells Canyon," *The Oregonian*, Aug. 15, 1995, 1.

Owens, Kenneth, "Pierce City Incident, 1885-1886," in Arif Dirlik, *Chinese on the American Frontier* (Lanham, Maryland: Rowman & Littlefield, 2001). Previously published in *Idaho Yesterdays* 3, No. 3 (Fall 1959).

Pfaelzer, Jean, *Driven Out, The Forgotten War Against Chinese Americans* (New York: Random House, 2007).

Rautenstrauch, Bill, "A Skeleton in the Closet," *Wallowa County Chieftain*, Enterprise, Oregon, February 16, 1995.

Schlesier, Karl H., *Aurora Crossing: A Novel of the Nez Perces* (Lubbock: Texas Tech University Press, 2008).

Simon-Smolinski, Carole, *Hells Canyon and the Middle Snake River: A Story of the Land and its People* (Lewiston, Idaho: Confluence Press, 2008).

Stratton, David H., "The Snake River Massacre of Chinese Miners, 1887," in *A Taste of the West* edited by Duane A. Smith (Boulder, Colorado: Pruett Publishing Co, 1983).

Sung, Betty Lee, *The Story of the Chinese in America* (New York: Macmillan Publishing Co, 1967).

Tansill, Charles Callan, *The Foreign Policy of Thomas F. Bayard, 1885-1897* (New York: Fordham University Press, 1940).

Treaty of Immigration between the United States and China, negotiated November 17, 1880. *Treaties and Other International Agreements of the United States of America, 1776-1949*, Volume No. 6, Department of State Publications (Washington, D.C.: U.S. Government Printing Office, 1971).

Treaty of Peace, Amity and Commerce between the United States and China, negotiated July 28, 1868. *Treaties and Other International Agreements of the United States of America, 1776-1949*, Volume No. 6, Department of State Publications (Washington, D.C.: U.S. Government Printing Office, 1971).

Trial Record, *State of Oregon vs. J. T. Canfield, Bruce Evans, L. O. LaRue, Hiram Maynard, Hezekiah Hughes, and Robert McMillan*, Office of Wallowa County Clerk, Wallowa County Courthouse, Enterprise, Oregon.

Tsai, Shih-shan Henry, *China and the Overseas Chinese in the United States, 1868-1911* (Fayetteville: University of Arkansas Press, 1983).

Tsai, Shih-shan Henry, *The Chinese Experience in America* (Bloomington and Indianapolis: Indiana University Press, 1986).

Tucker, Gerald J., "Massacre for Gold," *Old West Magazine* (Stillwater, Oklahoma: Western Publishing, Fall 1961).

Walla Walla Statesman, Walla Walla, Washington, September 30, 1891.

Wallowa County Chieftain, Joseph, Oregon, October 8, 1891, typewritten copy.

Wallowa County Court Docket, 1888-1898, and related documents, County Clerk's vault, Wallowa County Courthouse, Enterprise, Oregon.

Weathers, Ben, column, *Wallowa County Chieftain*, August 4, 1966, in collection of Weathers' columns, Wallowa County Museum, Joseph, Oregon.

Wegars, Priscilla, *The Ah Hee Diggings: Final Report of Archaeological Investigations at OR-GR-16, the Granite, Oregon "Chinese Walls Site,"* 1992-1994, (Moscow, University of Idaho Anthropological Reports, No. 97, 1995).

Wegars, Priscilla, *Chinese at the Confluence, Lewiston's Beuk Aie Temple* (Lewiston, Idaho: Confluence Press in Association with Lewis-Clark Center for Arts and History, 2000).

Wegars, Priscilla, *Chinese at the Confluence: Lewiston's Other Pioneers* (draft) (Moscow, Idaho: Archaelogical Research Consultants, 1992).

Wegars, Priscilla, *Uncovering a Chinese Legacy: Historical Archaeology at Centerville, Idaho* (Bureau of Land Management, U.S. Department of the Interior, 2001).

Welch, Ian, *Women's Work for Women: Women Missionaries in Nineteenth-Century China*, a paper submitted to the Eighth Women in Asia Conference at the University of Technology, Sydney, Australia, 2005.

Yung, Judy, Gordon H. Chang, and Him Mark Lai, *Chinese American Voices, From the Gold Rush to the Present* (Berkeley: University of California, 2006).

Index